GROUP DIFFERENCES IN ATTITUDES AND VOTES

A Study of the

1954 Congressional Election

by
Angus Campbell
and
Homer C. Cooper

GREENWOOD PRESS, PUBLISHERS
WESTPORT, CONNECTICUT

Library of Congress Cataloging in Publication Data

Campbell, Angus, 1910-
    Group differences in attitudes and votes.

    Reprint of the ed. published by the Survey Research
Center, University of Michigan, Ann Arbor, which was
issued as publication no. 15 of Survey Research Center
series.
    Includes bibliographical references.
    1. Voting--United States. 2. Social groups.
3. United States. Congress--Elections--1954.
I. Cooper, Homer Chassell, 1923-   joint author.
II. Title. III. Series: Michigan. University. Survey Research Center. Survey Research Center
series, publication no. 15.

[JK1853.C3 1974]   324.2'0973   73-21339
ISBN 0-8371-6185-1

The Institute for Social Research of the University of
Michigan is engaged in basic and applied research in the
social sciences. The Institute has two main research
units. The Survey Research Center is concerned with the
application of sample survey methods to the study of economic behavior, human relations in organizations, and
public attitudes and behavior in relation to public issues.
The Research Center for Group Dynamics studies the behavior of people in groups. The research is conducted in
industry, education, government and community life as
well as in the laboratory, in an effort to discover the de-
terminants of behavior, of group effectiveness and of human
satisfactions.
    Inquiries regarding the Institute and its research pro-
gram may be addressed to the Director of the Institute.

Copyright © by the University of Michigan, 1956

Originally published in 1956 by Survey Research Center,
Institute for Social Research, University of Michigan,
Ann Arbor

Reprinted with the permission of Institute for Social Research

Reprinted in 1974 by Greenwood Press,
a division of Williamhouse-Regency Inc.

Library of Congress Catalog Card Number 73-21339

ISBN 0-8371-6185-1

Printed in the United States of America

FOREWORD

This monograph is one of a series of publications, coming from the Survey Research Center of the University of Michigan, concerned with the political behavior of the American electorate. It presents the results of the third study of national elections undertaken by the Center since 1948.

All Survey Research Center studies depend on the skills and efforts of many people. The sample on which the present report is based was designed and selected by Dr. Leslie Kish and his staff in the Center's Sampling Section. The interviews were gathered by the Center's far-flung field staff, directed by Dr. Charles F. Cannell. The coding was supervised by Mrs. Jane S. Benjamin. Mrs. Evelyn Stewart, editor of Institute for Social Research publications, prepared the manuscript for printing. Mrs. Virginia D. Nye and Mrs. Marion T. Wirick provided essential secretarial services. The authors hope that all of these fellow members of the Center's staff will feel some satisfaction in this final product of their work.

CONTENTS

v

I

INTRODUCTION

The fact that major segments of the national electorate differ in their political attitudes and votes is one of the basic realities of this country's political life. Candidates are selected, platforms written and campaigns waged on the assumption that people of different economic, religious, ethnic, racial, occupational and regional status have characteristic political views and predilections. To a considerable degree the whole electoral process centers around a struggle for the favor of these large groups.

This "fundamental question of the relation between political attitude and social position"[1] has attracted the interest of many students of politics. The election statistics themselves are sufficient to show the biases of any segment of the population which can be associated with the political divisions from which votes are reported—states, districts, counties, or precincts. Thus, successive studies over the past thirty years have used election data to demonstrate the voting preferences of a variety of the major groups that make up the electorate.[2]

The first use of interview surveys in the study of voting behavior appears to have been made by Merriam and Gosnell[3] in their analysis of non-voting in Chicago in 1923. This pioneer study suggested something of the analytical power which the survey technique possesses when applied to the study of political behavior. In 1932 a major step forward was taken by

---

1. Tingsten, H., *Political Behavior*, London: P. S. King, 1937.
2. For a review of these studies see Eldersveld, S., Theory and Method in Voting Behavior Research, *J. of Politics*, *13*, 1951, 70-87.
3. Merriam, C. E. and Gosnell, H. F., *Non-Voting*, Chicago: University of Chicago Press, 1924, vii-287.

Robinson[1] who was able to demonstrate, through use of a national —although non-random—sample, that the major population groupings differed not only in their votes in the election of that year but also in their attitudes regarding a wide array of political issues. Similar findings were reported subsequently by the various polling agencies which came into prominence during the ensuing years.

The presidential election of 1940 provided the setting for the well-known study by Lazarsfeld, Berelson, and Gaudet[2] of the vote in Erie County, Ohio. This study brought to explicit focus the concept of group determination of the vote, placing particular emphasis on factors of religion, socio-economic status, and urban or rural residence. It also introduced the concept of "cross-pressures" resulting from overlapping group memberships, and showed their relation to political attitudes and votes. The 1948 study by Berelson, Lazarsfeld, and McPhee[3] of Elmira, New York, also was largely concerned with the implications of sociological setting on individual political behavior.

The first national study of the presidential vote based on probability sampling was carried out by the Survey Research Center[4] in the fall of 1948. This was a rather limited research undertaking, both in scope and in sample size, but it was sufficiently inclusive to provide a detailed record of the vote of most of the major population groups that make up the national electorate. In 1951 the Center explored the concept of "party identification" as an aspect of political motivation which had not been considered in the earlier studies.[5] In 1952 the Center undertook a more ambitious project, concerned primarily with the analysis of the motivational variables associated with participation and partisanship in the presidential election of that year.[6] This national survey also recorded the voting preferences of the important subgroups of the electorate.

1. Robinson, E. S., "Trends of the Voter's Mind," *Journal of Social Psychology*, 1933, *4*, 265-284.
2. Lazarsfeld, P., Berelson, B. and Gaudet, H., *The People's Choice*, New York: Columbia University Press, 1948.
3. Berelson, B., Lazarsfeld, P. and McPhee, W., *Voting*, Chicago· University of Chicago Press, 1954.
4. Campbell, A. and Kahn, R. L., *The People Elect a President*, Ann Arbor: Institute for Social Research, 1952.
5. Belknap, G. and Campbell, A., "Political Party Identification and Attitudes toward Foreign Policy," *Public Opinion Quarterly*, 1952, *15*, 601-623.
6. Campbell, A., Gurin, G., and Miller, W. E., *The Voter Decides*, Evanston: Row, Peterson & Co., 1954.

In the fall of 1954 the Center had a limited opportunity to extend its inquiries into the behavior of the national electorate. In October that year we were preparing to conduct one of our periodic economic surveys and it was possible to add to the questionnaire a few questions of a political nature.

Within this severely limited scope we could not carry forward the study of "intervening variables" on which our 1952 study had concentrated. It was feasible, however, to obtain data which would make possible a more detailed analysis than had previously been available on a national scale of the relationship of group membership to voting preferences and to attitudes regarding political issues and personalities.

The present report, therefore, focuses primarily on group differences in political attitudes and in voting. The groups we are considering are not the various face-to-face membership groups to which most Americans belong but the broad population categories which make up the national electorate. These include not only the basic socio-economic, religious, and racial groupings but also labor unions and political parties. These large social aggregates are not "groups" in the narrow sense of the term, although they are commonly referred to as such in political discussion. We will use the term "population groups" in the present report in order to imply the broad dispersed character of the social categories we are considering. Similarly, the term "membership" as we are using it merely implies inclusion in the particular population group in question. Only in the case of political parties are we able to speak of sense or degree of group identification.

Because our study was so restricted in the number of questions that could be asked, we had to represent broad issues of policies and personalities with a single question—never a desirable procedure. Moreover, we were unable to get a post-election report of the respondents' votes and had to rely on their pre-election statements of intention. This necessitated a procedure of correction which will be discussed in the ensuing pages. These are demerits for which the reader will have to make allowance; they were unavoidable within the resources available.

Fortunately we do not have to apologize for the sample on which the data of this report are based. Although it was not large (1139 cases) it was drawn by the Center's highly developed methods of probability sampling. Within the limits of sampling error it represents the adult population living in private households in the United States at the time of the survey. The

3

sampling errors of all the data can be calculated and the reader may inform himself as to the reliability of the difference between any two percentages given by referring to the Appendix on the Sample in the back of this report.

The reader will find that the data of this study are reported in much fuller detail than is usually possible in printed publications. This is done because some of the conclusions drawn from the study require reference to a wide range of tables. In order to lighten the burden for the reader, however, many of these tables are deferred to the Appendix.

II

THE OBJECTIVES AND THE VARIABLES

Our study has two general objectives. One is to provide a description of the political acts and attitudes of the major population groups in the congressional election of 1954. The other is to ascertain such relationships as our data may reveal between the characteristics of these groups and the nature of their political behavior.

Descriptive analysis has significance only insofar as the event being described has significance. It is our belief that the national elections in the United States are sufficiently important to warrant description as specific events, especially if such description is systematically repeated so that the analysis of successive elections becomes possible. Inasmuch as the present study follows two earlier studies of presidential elections carried out by the Survey Research Center, the descriptive data from the 1954 election have more than ordinary interest.

To go beyond the specifically descriptive aspects of our data we must represent in conceptual terms the properties of the groups we are studying and the basic character of the behavior they express. On the basis of such hypotheses as seem promising we will then examine the interaction of these two sets of variables.

We begin with the assumption that the population groups we are studying will vary in the extent to which they differ politically from the electorate at large. Some may have no distinguishing characteristics politically; others may differ greatly in some particular attribute; others may have a pattern of attitudes and behaviors that distinguishes them from the rest.

5

We assume further that a population group may acquire
political individuality through either of two mechanisms. It may
come about coincidentally through the fact that many individual
members of the group are reacting similarly but independently
to some outside factor which affects them differently·than it does
the rest of the population.   Thus, if a hard-pressed federal administration were to levy a special head tax on all Americans
of Scottish descent, there would undoubtedly be a wide-spread
reaction of disapproval among such people.   In such a case, the
group itself has no effect on the membership but a group position is created by the independent responses of the individual
members.[1]

A group position may also come about as the result of direct
group influence on the membership. Groups having high membership identification, that is, groups to which the individual
members feel a strong attachment, have the power to affect the
behavior of their members. These "group effects," resulting
from the wish — conscious or not — of individual members to
conform to the standards they perceive their group to hold, have
been the subject of much interest in the study of small face-to-
face groups.[2]   We assume that a similar phenomenon may occur
in connection with the larger population groups, provided that the
essential relationships between the individual and the group are
present.

These underlying suppositions lead us to a series of hypotheses regarding group differences:

1. Groups having high membership identification and strong
   group standards in the area of politics will be the most
   distinctive in their political characteristics.

2. Groups of high membership identification but without
   group standards regarding political attitudes or behavior,
   and groups of low membership identification will not be
   politically distinctive unless there is some outside factor
   which evokes a common coincidental response from the
   group's members.

---

1. Contrary to a statement by Berelson et al, we do not believe
that "Contact is a condition for consensus," at least not as we understand the term "consensus."
   2. See Cartwright, D. and Zander, A., *Group Dynamics, Research and
Theory*, Evanston: Row, Peterson & Co. , 1953.

6

3. In groups of high membership identification and strong group standards of political behavior, those members with strongest group identification will be most politically distinctive.

4. Overlapping group membership will result in either reinforcement or diminution of the partisan characteristics of the original groups, assuming both groups have partisan characteristics and depending on whether these characteristics are congruent or in conflict.

Unfortunately our data are not adequate to test all these hypotheses fully. However, we will keep them in mind as we examine the data which are presented in the following chapters and return to a discussion of them in the concluding chapter. The specific measures which were used to obtain the data are described below.

THE VARIABLES

To accomplish the purposes of the study it was necessary to assemble three types of information from each of our 1139 respondents. We needed to know (1) how each respondent voted in the 1954 congressional election, (2) how he stood on the political issues important at the time and (3) what population groups he belonged to.

The Vote

As we have stated in the Introduction, the interviews on which this study is based were taken in October 1954, just prior to the congressional election. We did not have a post-election re-interview and consequently do not have a direct report from the respondents as to whether they voted and, if so, for whom. In order to compare our 1954 data with the voting data from 1948 and 1952, however, it is necessary to convert our reports of intention into estimates of probable voting behavior.

We know from our earlier studies that a simple pre-election statement of intention to vote cannot be accepted at face value as a predictor of ultimate voting behavior. Typically a considerably higher proportion of respondents say they expect to vote than actually get to the polls. Our present study has proved no exception to this rule. When our respondents were asked in October: "Do you expect to vote in the election next month, or do you think you probably will not vote?", 69 percent of them answered that they expected to vote, whereas the ratio of total House of Representatives vote to the census estimate of adult population in November 1954 indicates that only about 42 percent of the adult population actually voted.

The fact that a large proportion of respondents who intend to vote fail to go to the polls seriously distorts estimates of turnout; it also introduces a partisan bias in the estimated vote. By comparing respondents' pre-election statements of intention to vote with their post-election reports of vote or of failure to vote, the 1948 and 1952 Survey Research Center studies found that in both elections the group of intenders who failed to vote contained a higher proportion of Democrats than was true of the group of intenders who actually voted. If we assume that the same was true of the pre-election data of the 1954 study, then we should expect that the use of the "intention-to-vote" report without qualifying criteria would over-state the actual turnout and over-estimate the Democratic vote.

In order to overcome these weaknesses of the "intention–to–vote" measure it was necessary to "correct" this raw intention score by the use of some other information regarding the intenders which might be assumed to be correlated with the probability of actual vote. Following the simple logic of persistence, the obvious basis of correction would be the frequency of voting in previous elections. In order to obtain this information we asked our respondents if they had voted in previous national and state elections and, if so, how often.

Our assignments of probable vote or non-vote were made on the basis of responses to the following three questions:

"In the national and state elections since you have been old enough to vote would you say you have voted in all of them, most of them, some of them, or none of them?"

"Do you expect to vote in the election next month or do you think you probably will not vote?"

"Of the two candidates for Congress (Representative) which one do you think you will vote for?"

Our 1139 respondents were classified as probable voters or probable non-voters according to the following specifications:

8

Probable Democratic Voters: Have voted in all or most past elections for which eligible, intend to vote in 1954, will vote Democratic for Congress.

Probable Republican Voters: Have voted in all or most past elections for which eligible, intend to vote in 1954, will vote Republican for Congress.

Probable Non-Voters: Any one of the following—have voted in some or none of past elections for which eligible, or will not vote or do not know whether will vote in 1954, or undecided for whom to vote for Congress.

As Table II-1 demonstrates, these definitions divided our sample into 24 percent probable Democratic voters, 22 percent probable Republican voters, and 54 percent probable non-voters. The division among voters alone was 52 percent Democratic and 48 percent Republican. A comparison of the survey with the official returns shows that our definitions not only procured approximately the right proportions of voters to non-voters, but that the voters obtained also gave as their vote intentions proportions which are quite close to the true Democratic-Republican vote division in 1954. (And if we were to subtract from the 100 million adults of voting age the several million non-voting adults in institutions, transients, and members of the Armed Forces included in the census figure but not sampled by our survey, the proportions of voters to non-voters in our sample would be even closer to the official figures.)[1]

Our confidence in this method of assignment is considerably strengthened by the results obtained when we apply the same procedure to the data of our 1952 study. In that survey a similar question regarding previous voting was asked. By using a similar although less severe screening process a proportion of "probable voters" comparable to the actual voting turnout of that year can be selected. When the post-election voting reports of these "probable voters" are checked we find that 92 percent of them reported having voted. Of those, five percent reported switching their vote from their pre-election choice to the other candidate—about equal numbers in each direction. Of the "probable voters" 57 percent intended to vote for Eisenhower; of the actual voters 58 percent voted for Eisenhower.

---

1. See *The Voter Decides,* page 4, for a discussion of this discrepancy between survey and census populations.

Table II-1

COMPARISON OF "PROBABLE VOTE" ACCORDING TO SURVEY
FINDINGS WITH OFFICIAL ELECTION RETURNS FOR
1954 VOTE FOR HOUSE OF REPRESENTATIVES

Total sample or all U.S. adults	"Probable vote" from survey	Actual vote from official returns
Democratic voters	24%	22.1%
Republican voters	22	20.0
Other party voters	--	0.4
Non-voters	54	57.5
	100%	100.0%
Total sample and census estimate	1139	100,223,000

Voters only	"Probable vote" from survey	Actual vote from official returns
Democratic voters	52%	52.1%
Republican voters	48	47.0
Other voters	--	0.9
	100%	100.0%
"Probable voters" and official vote total	523	42,579,977

We cannot assume, of course, that the correspondence between "probable voters" and actual voters would be as high in
every national election as it apparently was in 1952. Our 1948
data indicate that the relationship in that year would have been
less close. There is reason to believe, however, that a congressional election would be less subject than a presidential
election to discrepancies resulting from the activation of infrequent voters and late switching from one candidate to another.

In any case, it is apparent that our procedure of selecting "probable voters" has certain errors implicit in it. If we were interested in the analysis of individual voters these errors would be a matter of serious concern. Since this report deals entirely with population groups, however, it does not appear that our analysis can be seriously biased by our use of "probable" rather than actual voters.

Issues

While the vote may be regarded as the ultimate act of political behavior, the positions the electorate take on the important issues of the day are in some respects a more interesting area for political analysis. The categorical character of the vote disguises much of the complex interplay of political factors which lies behind the voter's choice. The study of issues illuminates these areas of perception and attitude and makes possible a more penetrating analysis of the citizen's political life-space.

The range of issues which might be the subject of inquiry is of course very broad. Our selection was purely judgmental. The questions we asked were intended to meet the objectives of this particular study and cannot be thought of as representing the entire range of possible questions that might have been asked. Eight questions were asked of our 1139 respondents, covering a variety of political subjects.

The first issue area concerned the performance of the Republican Party in its two years of tenure in Washington. Each respondent was asked two open-ended questions pertaining to the activities of the new administration. They read as follows:

"What would you say is the best thing the Republican party has done since it took over the government two years ago?"

"What would you say is the worst thing the Republican party has done in the last two years?"

The second issue area concerned the performance of President Eisenhower. The first of the two questions pertaining directly to the President requested an absolute judgment in terms of satisfaction or dissatisfaction with his activity in office. The second asked the respondents to compare Mr. Eisenhower's performance with that of previous presidents. The questions read:

"Has Mr. Eisenhower turned out to be as good a president as you thought he would or have you been disappointed in him?"

"Would you say Mr. Eisenhower has been a better-than-average president, just about average, or not as good as average?"

The fifth question inquired into the respondents' expectations concerning the effect of the election outcome on their personal financial situation. This same question had been asked in our 1952 survey.

"Do you think it will make any difference in how you and your family get along financially whether the Democrats or Republicans win?"

One question was then asked about foreign affairs. It concerned the relationship of the United States to the other nations of the world. We had also asked this question in our 1948 and 1952 surveys.

"Some people think that since the end of the last world war this country has gone too far in concerning itself with problems in other parts of the world. How do you feel about this?"

The next question asked the respondents their opinions concerning the degree to which the Federal Government should undertake social legislation. The wording was identical with that of a question asked in our 1952 survey. It read as follows:

"Some people think the national government should do more in trying to deal with such problems as unemployment, education, housing, and so on. Others think that the government is already doing too much. On the whole would you say that what the government is doing is about right, too much, or not enough?"

The last of the issue questions dealt with Senator Joseph R. McCarthy. The senator had been a highly controversial figure during the year preceding our study and our respondents were asked to indicate their reaction to him. This was done indirectly by proposing a hypothetical election situation in which the senator was proposed to be supporting a particular candidate. The question was stated in the following terms:

12

"If you knew that Senator McCarthy was supporting a candidate for Congress, would you be more likely to vote for that candidate, or less likely, or wouldn't it make any difference to you?"

These eight questions provided the data which we will use in our analysis of differences between population groups in their stands on political issues. It is not an inclusive list by any means; we would have preferred a much more detailed questionnaire. The questions were asked in the order in which they have been presented here. The distributions of answers are shown in the "total" columns of the appropriate tables in Chapter III.

Population Group Membership

As we have seen in the Introduction, the analysis of the voting of the major population groups is a familiar procedure both for practical politicians and for academic scholars. The groups which are most commonly considered are those differing in sex, age, race, religion, education, income, occupation, location, and ethnic background. All of these variables are included in our present study except ethnic background, the ethnic groups being too small in most cases to be reliably represented in a sample of 1139 respondents. We have also included two additional variables which have particular political significance. They are labor union membership and political party identification.

The questions which were used to place our respondents in their proper population groups are given below. Except for occupation, labor union affiliation, and income, the characteristics recorded are those of the respondent, not of other members of the family.

The *sex* and *race* of the respondent were recorded by the interviewer after the interview was completed. *Age* was determined by the question, "What year were you born?" The respondent's *religious preference* was obtained by the question, "Is your church preference Protestant, Catholic, or Jewish?"

The *communities* in which the respondents lived were classified into three types—metropolitan, cities and towns, and rural. Seven metropolitan communities (over one million in population) were included in the sample. The definition of metropolitan included the central city, suburbs of 50,000 and over, suburbs

DISTRIBUTIONS OF THE POPULATION GROUPS

Sex		Education	
Men	47%	Grade school	37%
Women	53	High school	45
	100%	College	18
			100%

Age		Occupation of family head	
		Professional - technical	7%
21-24	6%	Business - managerial	14
25-34	26	Clerical	5
35-44	22	Sales	4
45-54	21	Skilled labor	30
55-64	12	Unskilled labor	13
Over 64	13	Farm operator	9
	100%	Retired	9
		Housewife	5
Religion		Unemployed	3
		Other	1
Protestant	75%		100%
Catholic	19		
Jewish	3	Labor union member in family	
Other or none	3	Member	28%
	100%	No member	71
		Not ascertained	1
Race			100%
White	90%	Total family income	
Negro	9	Under $1000	8%
Other	1	$1000-1999	11
	100%	$2000-2999	12
		$3000-3999	17
		$4000-4999	13
Type of community		$5000-5999	13
		$6000-7499	9
Metropolitan center	15%	$7500-9999	6
Metropolitan suburb	13	$10,000 or more	7
City or town	53	Not ascertained	4
Open country	19		100%
	100%		

of 2,500 to 50,000, and rural suburbs in the metropolitan area. Central cities and suburbs are reported separately in some of the tables of this report. The category of cities and towns included cities of 50,000 or over (but not more than one million), cities of 2,500 to 50,000, and rural towns and congested areas under 2,500. The rural category included only rural blocks and open country.

Education was determined by the following series of questions: "How many grades of school did you finish?" If the answer was more than eight, the respondent was asked, "Have you had any schooling other than high school?" If he said yes, "What other schooling have you had?" If he said he had attended college, he was asked, "Do you have a college degree?" In our present analysis the respondent's education was classified as grade, high, or college. The category "grade" included those persons who did not attend school at all or who attended no more than eight grades. "High school" included those who completed or had some high school and who may or may not have had further non-academic training. "College" included those who had college degrees or who attended college but were not graduated.

The *occupation of the family head* was classified according to the following questions: "What is your (the head of the house's) occupation? I mean, what kind of work do you do?" If employed, "Do you work for yourself or for someone else?" If unemployed, "What kind of work do you usually do?" If retired, "What kind of work did you do before you retired?"

In general, the responses to the above questions were coded into the standard categories listed in the *Alphabetical Index of Occupations and Industries* published by the Bureau of the Census, U. S. Department of Commerce and based on the 1950 Census of Population. In our system of classification the business-managerial category consisted of self-employed businessmen and artisans; managers, officials, and proprietors; and farm managers. Skilled labor included craftsmen, foremen, and kindred workers; and operatives and kindred workers. Unskilled labor included laborers, service workers, and farm laborers. The other categories are relatively self-evident. In all cases the occupation used was that of the family head, whether that individual was our respondent or not.

The *labor union affiliation* of the head or respondent was obtained by answers to the questions: "Do either you (or other member of your family) belong to a labor union?" If necessary,

"Who is it that belongs?" The respondent was classified as a union member if either the head or the respondent (if not the head), or both, belonged to a union. All kinds of labor unions were included—professional and other white-collar as well as industrial.

The total *family income* was determined by the following questions: "The next question applies to all the members of your family. Could you tell me how much you and your family expect to be making this year, 1954; I mean, your entire income before taxes during the calendar year 1954?.... Does that include the income of everyone in the family?" In case of question, the "family" was defined as persons living within the respondent's dwelling unit whom he considered to be members of his family.

Identification with political parties is a concept in which the Survey Research Center has a strong and continuing interest. We have defined party identification in our earlier studies[1] as the sense of personal attachment or belonging which an individual feels toward a given political party. The concept is perceptual, not behavioral, in that it is based on the degree to which the respondents perceive themselves as belonging to political parties, rather than upon the frequencies of various types of political participation in which they might have engaged. The specific questions asked to measure this variable were: "Generally speaking, in politics, do you usually think of yourself as a Republican, a Democrat, an Independent, or what?" If the respondent's answer was "Republican" or "Democrat": "Would you call yourself a strong (Republican or Democrat) or a not very strong (Republican or Democrat)?" If his answer was "Independent": "Do you think of yourself as closer to the Republican or Democratic party?"

It will be observed that in contrast to the questions regarding the other population groups those regarding political parties asked the respondent not only to place himself in the proper party category but also to indicate his degree of attachment to the party of his choice. On the basis of his responses to the first and second or first and third questions above, each respondent was classified under one of the headings of Table II-3. Somewhat less than half of our respondents called themselves strong or weak Democrats, whereas a little more than a quarter identified themselves as strong or weak Republicans. Approximately one fifth of the population classified themselves as

---

1. A fuller discussion of the concept of party identification appears in *The Voter Decides*, Chapter V.

Independents. A very few respondents were so non-political that no such party classification could be made.[1]

The characteristics of these different party groups will be reviewed in detail in Chapters IV and VI. However, it is useful at this point to observe the high stability of the distributions of party identification reported in Survey Research Center studies between 1952 and 1954. The three samples reported in Table II-3 were drawn from the national population by similar methods at year intervals. It is apparent that there was virtually no change in the proportions of péople giving themselves the different party labels during that time.

Our data do not tell us, of course, if any of our respondents changed their political labels from one year to the next. It is reasonable to assume that some did. Such shifting as may have occurred appears to have been random and therefore compensating. It is of interest that, despite the change in the Federal

Table II-3

PARTY IDENTIFICATION

Party identification	October 1952	September 1953	October 1954
Strong Democrat	22%	22%	22%
Weak Democrat	25	23	25
Independent Democrat	10	8	9
Independent	5	4	7
Independent Republican	7	6	6
Weak Republican	14	15	14
Strong Republican	13	15	13
Apolitical, don't know	4	7	4
	100%	100%	100%
Number of cases	1614	1023	1139

1. In considering these and subsequent data regarding party identification the reader must keep in mind that approximately 30 percent of our national sample is located in the Southern States and that in the South Democrats, as we define them, outnumber Republicans more than four to one.

Government in 1952 and the concurrent rejuvenation of the Republican party, there was no shift of public loyalties toward the Republican party during the period between October 1952 and October 1954. We know very little about how party identification is created or how it is changed. Our data show us, however, that if there was any conversion of Democrats or Independents to the Republican fold during the first two years of the Eisenhower administration, the loss was fully replaced by movements in the other direction.

We will see in later chapters that party identification, as we have conceived and measured it, is one of the most powerful variables we have available for the analysis of political behavior. Not only is it more meaningful psychologically than such traditional variables as education, age, income and the like; it also has greater ability to order political data. It is not a new concept; politicians have thought in such terms since time out of mind. It is relatively new to quantitative analysis, however. Because we feel that this variable has not been given adequate attention in earlier studies of political behavior our measure of party identification is given considerable prominence in this report.

III

THE VOTES OF THE POPULATION GROUPS

The first step in our analysis of the political implications of membership in the major population groups is a comparison of their voting records.

Chapter III describes the population characteristics of the 1954 vote. This description is given increased depth and meaning by the inclusion in the tables of this chapter of comparable data from our 1948 and 1952 studies. A word of warning is necessary concerning these three sets of data. The 1954 study differs from the 1948 and 1952 studies in two important respects: First, the 1954 study refers to total House of Representatives vote, whereas the 1948 and 1952 studies considered total presidential vote. Second, the 1954 tables use "probable vote" (as defined in Chapter II) obtained from pre-election interviews, whereas the 1948 and 1952 tables deal with "actual vote" as reported during post-election interviews. These differences must be kept in mind while interpreting the meaning of the comparisons.

In the 1948 post-election study, the classification of a respondent as a "voter" or "non-voter" and the determination as to which presidential candidate he voted for depended upon his answers to the following two questions:

"In this election about half the people voted and half of them didn't. Did you vote?"

(If "yes"): "Whom did you vote for?"

In the 1952 post-election study the following version was used:

"In talking to people about the election, we find that a lot of people weren't able to vote because they weren't registered, or they were sick, or they just didn't have the time. How about you, did you vote this time?"

(If "yes"): "Whom did you vote for for president?"

In both these studies, as in the 1954 study, the questions pertaining to voting were worded in such a way as to avoid the implication that failure to vote meant dereliction of duty, and to relieve any embarrassment resulting from voting for the losing candidate.

Keeping in mind the definitions of "voters" and "non-voters" for the elections of 1948, 1952, and 1954, we are ready to compare the voting records of the groups in which we are interested and to consider the shifts which took place in these three elections.

Men and Women

Table III-1 shows that in 1954 men gave a substantial majority of votes to Democratic candidates for Congress, whereas a small majority of women's votes went to Republicans. In each of the 1948, 1952, and 1954 elections larger proportions of women than men voted Republican. As we will see later this persistent discrepancy apparently derives from socio-economic factors underlying the vote, women in those social categories most heavily Democratic being less likely to vote than women in the categories which are predominantly Republican.

As might be expected the proportion of women reporting not voting is higher than that of men in all three elections. Because of the fact that there are more women than men in the adult population the contribution of the two sexes to the actual vote is about equal and varies only slightly from one election to the next. The women's vote made up 51 percent of the total in 1948, 51 percent in ˙1952 and 48 percent in 1954.

Age

In Table III-2 we find a steady increase in the proportion of votes going to Republican candidates as we move from the youngest to the oldest group. Table III-3 compares various age groups for the 1948, 1952 and 1954 elections. For each election it will be noticed that as age increases the ratio of Republican to Democratic voters increases.

20

Table III-1

VOTING BEHAVIOR OF MEN AND WOMEN IN THREE ELECTIONS

	Men			Women		
	1948	1952	1954	1948	1952	1954
Voted for: **						
Democrat	36%	34%	30%	29%	28%	19%
Republican	28	44	23	26	41	22
Other	1	1	--	2	*	--
Not ascertained	4	--	--	3	--	--
Did not vote	31	21	47	40	31.	59
Not ascertained	*	--	--	*	--	--
	100%	100%	100%	100%	100%	100%
Number of cases	303	738	532	356	876	607

*The asterisk is used to denote less than one-half of one percent in this and all succeeding tables.

**In this and all succeeding tables "voted for" in the 1948 and 1952 columns refers to actual presidential vote as reported in post-election interviews; in 1954, to "probable vote" in the House of Representatives vote.

TableI II-2

RELATION OF AGE TO PROBABLE 1954 VOTE

	21-24	25-34	35-44	45-54	55-64	65 & over
Probable vote:						
Democratic	14%	23%	27%	27%	24%	22%
Republican	9	14	22	30	27	27
Probable non-voter	77	63	51	43	49	51
	100%	100%	100%	100%	100%	100%
Number of cases	74	292	247	238	135	146

Table III-3

RELATION OF AGE TO VOTING BEHAVIOR IN THREE ELECTIONS

	21-34			35-44			45-54			55 & over		
	1948	1952	1954	1948	1952	1954	1948	1952	1954	1948	1952	1954
Voted for:												
Democrat	32%	31%	21%	38%	34%	27%	33%	33%	27%	27%	27%	23%
Republican	18	37	13	24	41	22	37	45	30	31	48	27
Other	2	*	--	1	1	--	3	1	--	2	2	--
Not ascertained	3	--	--	3	--	--	2	--	--	5	--	--
Did not vote	44	32	66	33	24	51	25	21	43	37	23	50
Not ascertained	1	--	--	1	--	--	--	--	--	*	--	--
	100%	100%	100%	100%	100%	100%	100%	100%	100%	100%	100%	100%
Number of cases	198	485	366	174	381	247	126	284	238	156	442	281

A second point of interest is that in each election the 45-54 age group has the smallest proportion of non-voters and that the 21-34 age group has the largest proportion.

The data suggest that the motives that impel the individual voter to the polls are weakest during the first years of his eligibility, that they increase as he matures into middle age and its attendant responsibilities, and that they weaken again as he moves into his later years.

Religion

We see in Table III-4 that in 1954 the Protestant vote was evenly split between Republican and Democratic candidates. The greater tendencies of Catholics and Jews to vote Democratic contributed to the Democratic victory. Table III-4 also demonstrates that the Catholic vote, which had been two-to-one Democratic in 1948, fell to an even division in 1952 and then returned to a sizable Democratic majority in 1954. Also to be noticed in Table III-6 is the fact that in each election a higher proportion of Catholics than Protestants voted.

Table III-4

RELATION OF RELIGION TO VOTING BEHAVIOR
IN THREE ELECTIONS

	Protestant			Catholic			Jewish[1]	
	1948	1952	1954	1948	1952	1954	1952	1954
Voted for:								
Democrat	25%	26%	22%	49%	43%	33%	64%	32%
Republican	28	45	22	25	41	23	27	21
Other	2	1	--	*	1	--	2	--
Not ascertained	2	--	--	5	--	--	--	--
Did not vote	43	28	56	20	15	44	7	47
Not ascertained	*	--	--	1	--	--	--	--
	100%	100%	100%	100%	100%	100%	100%	100%
Number of cases	461	1156	857	140	343	216	45	34

[1] The Jewish sample in 1948 was not large enough to justify consideration.

It must be kept in mind that the division of the electorate into religious categories is contaminated by important related factors. The relatively high turnout of Catholics, for example, is undoubtedly influenced by the fact that most Catholics live in urban centers in the North—communities in which the turnout of all groups is relatively high. Conversely, the Protestant record is depressed by the fact that this group includes most Negroes and most southerners, both groups with poor voting records.

Table III-5 shows that the Negro vote in 1954 was heavily Democratic, much more so than the white vote. The all-over effect of the Negro vote is limited of course by the fact that Negroes constitute only one-tenth of the total population and four-fifths of them failed to vote in 1954. In contrast, approximately half of the much larger white population turned out and voted.

Table III-5

RELATION OF RACE TO VOTING BEHAVIOR IN THREE ELECTIONS

	White			Negro		
	1948	1952	1954	1948	1952	1954
Voted for:						
Democrat	33%	31%	25%	18%	26%	15%
Republican	29	47	24	10	6	6
Other	2	1	--	*	1	--
Not ascertained	2	--	--	8	--	--
Did not vote	33	21	51	64	67	79
Not ascertained	1	--	--	*	--	--
	100%	100%	100%	100%	100%	100%
Number of cases	585	1453	1022	61	157	103

In all three of the elections under comparison a higher proportion of the Negro than white vote was Democratic. Negro support of the Democratic presidential candidate in the Republican year of 1952 is striking; Negroes were one of the very few population groups that did not shift toward Eisenhower. This adherence of the Negro voters to the Democratic party presents a very interesting example of reversal in the political orientation of an important population group. The Negro voter, once firmly attached to the Republican party by the events associated with abolition and the Civil War, is now, a hundred years later, one of the most dependable supporters of the Democratic standard. We will return to this question of group change at the end of this chapter.

Type of Community

The division of party votes in areas of different population density is given in Table III-6. Perhaps the most interesting feature of this table is the contrast in party preferences in the metropolitan centers and their suburban areas, with the former clearly Democratic and the latter strongly Republican. The increased Republican strength in the suburbs in 1952 was noted by Harris[1] with the suggestion that people moving to the suburbs were being converted into Republicans by the Republican atmosphere they found there. There is reason to believe, however, that most of the Republican gain in the suburbs is due to the fact that most of the people who move to the suburbs are Republicans before they arrive there.

Table III-6

RELATION OF TYPE OF COMMUNITY TO
PROBABLE 1954 VOTE

	Metro centers	Metro suburbs	City or town	Open country
Probable vote:				
Democratic	26%	22%	25%	20%
Republican	21	31	23	15
Probable non-voter	53	47	52	65
	100%	100%	100%	100%
Number of cases	169	150	601	219

While the metropolitan vote (as we define it) is exclusively northern, the smaller-city and rural votes include the South. This contributes a higher Democratic weighting to these two columns than we would find if the Southern vote were omitted. It should be remarked that only about half of the rural residents can be classified as farmers and, as we shall see in Table III-9, farmers were more likely to vote Republican in 1954 than were rural non-farmers.

Table III-7 presents comparative data for the 1948, 1952 and 1954 elections. The metropolitan areas (centers and suburbs combined) voted heavily Democratic in 1948, substantially

1. Harris, L., *Is There a Republican Majority?*, New York: Harper and Bros., 1954.

25

Table III-7

RELATION OF TYPE OF COMMUNITY TO VOTING BEHAVIOR IN THREE ELECTIONS

	Metropolitan area			City or town			Open country		
	1948	1952	1954	1948	1952	1954	1948	1952	1954
Voted for:									
Democrat	46%	33%	24%	27%	31%	25%	24%	25%	20%
Republican	32	44	25	30	42	23	12	42	15
Other	1	2	--	1	*	--	3	1	--
Not ascertained	4	--	--	3	--	--	1	--	--
Did not vote	17	21	51	38	27	52	59	32	65
Not ascertained	--	--	--	1	--	--	1	--	--
	100%	100%	100%	100%	100%	100%	100%	100%	100%
Number of cases	181	438	319	354	928	601	127	248	219

Republican in 1952, and about even in 1954. Cities and towns were near an even balance in 1948, swung strongly Republican in 1952, but returned to an even division in 1954. Rural areas were sharply Democratic in 1948, equally sharply Republican in 1952, but Democratic again in 1954.

As for voting turnout, the trend over three elections is that of higher voting rates as community size increases. People living in the open country have clearly the poorest voting record over this period, although the increase in their turnout in 1952 over 1948 was remarkable.

Education

Table III-8 presents the probable 1954 votes of people of different educational status. Voters with less than a college education voted Democratic in 1954, whereas those voters who attended college preferred the Republicans. Also to be noted is that a higher percentage of the college-educated went to the polls. Although a higher proportion of the college-educated voted, the total vote of the grade and high school populations was considerably larger, since as Table II-2 indicates, less than one-fifth of our adult population has attended college.

If we divide the sample into different income brackets and look at the votes of people of different educational levels within each bracket (Table B-1),[1] the college-educated are found to have

---

1. All tables labelled with the letter B are in the Appendix.

Table III-8

RELATION OF EDUCATION TO VOTING BEHAVIOR
IN THREE ELECTIONS

	Grade School			High School			College		
	1948	1952	1954	1948	1952	1954	1948	1952	1954
Voted for:									
Democrat	35%	30%	22%	34%	34%	25%	17%	24%	25%
Republican	16	31	16	29	46	22	55	65	35
Other	1	1	--	1	*	--	3	1	--
Not ascertained	3	--	--	3	--	--	5	--	--
Did not vote	44	38	62	33	20	53	20	10	40
Not ascertained	1	--	--	*	--	--	--	--	--
	100%	100%	100%	100%	100%	100%	100%	100%	100%
Number of cases	293	660	416	266	712	517	99	238	202

been the most Republican at all income levels while those voters with high or grade school education showed a Republican majority only if they fell in the upper-income brackets. Non-college persons with incomes less than $6000 gave substantial margins to Democrats. When labor union membership is controlled (Table B-2), the data suggest that the size of the margin given to Democrats by union members was independent of educational level, but that non-members changed from a slight Democratic majority to a substantial Republican majority as educational attainment changed from grade to college level.

When community size is controlled (Table B-3), the data show that in metropolitan areas and in cities and towns the proportion of the Republican vote increased as education increased, but that in rural areas the vote remained slightly Democratic regardless of the educational level reached.[1]

The correlation of education with party preference also appeared in both of our earlier studies. It is one expression of the general tendency of higher-status population groups to support the Republican party. Succeeding tables give other evidences of this same aspect of American political life.

---

1. The failure of rural voting preferences to correlate with this and other demographic variables is consistent with the findings of Duncan MacRae, Jr. reported in "Occupations and the Congressional Vote," 1940-1950, *American Sociological Review*, June, 1955. *20*, 3, 332-340.

It is a matter of interest that the educational differences in party choice were sharper in 1948 than they were in either 1952 or 1954. This is also true of the other class-related variables (income, occupation, union membership). It appears that the 1948 election was more "class-angled" so far as the voters were concerned than either of the other two, no doubt reflecting the different issues and personalities involved in the different years.

High-education people not only vote more Republican; they vote more often. The relation of turnout to educational level is clear in all three elections. It is interesting, however, that the variations in turnout from year to year do not differ greatly from one educational group to another.

Occupation of Family Head

The occupation of the family head is also an important correlate of voting (Table III-9). Respondents belonging to professional, business or managerial, and sales families voted Republican to varying degrees in 1954, whereas skilled and unskilled labor and the unemployed voted Democratic. Farmers and clerical personnel divided their votes between the two parties.

Table III-10 shows that professional and managerial people voted heavily Republican in the 1948, 1952, and 1954 elections, but that the trend of their vote has been toward reduced Republican majorities. The remaining white-collar vote did not favor either party in 1948 or 1954 although along with most other demographic groups it swung to Eisenhower in 1952. Skilled labor, on the other hand, has consistently produced Democratic majorities, but those of 1952 and 1954 were light compared with that of 1948. Unskilled labor recorded Democratic majorities of a fairly constant size in all three elections. The farm population has varied more than any of the other groups; in 1948 it voted Democratic by a substantial margin, in 1952 it supported the Republicans even more impressively, and in 1954 farmers came back to an even division.

Labor Union Affiliation

The "Total population" columns of Table III-11 show that union members and members of their families voted heavily Democratic in 1954, whereas families without a union member gave a majority of their votes to Republican candidates.

28

Table III-9

RELATION OF OCCUPATION OF FAMILY HEAD TO PROBABLE 1954 VOTE

	Professional and technical	Business and managerial	Clerical	Sales	Skilled labor	Un- skilled labor	Farm operators	Retired	Un- employed
Probable vote:									
Democratic	18%	24%	29%	14%	26%	26%	22%	27%	24%
Republican	27	35	26	25	19	10	23	28	9
Probable non-voter	55	41	45	61	55	64	55	45	67
	100%	100%	100%	100%	100%	100%	100%	100%	100%
Number of cases	84	162	58	44	337	144	104	100	33

Table III-10

RELATION OF OCCUPATION OF HEAD OF FAMILY TO VOTING BEHAVIOR IN THREE ELECTIONS

	Professional and managerial			Other white collar			Skilled and semi-skilled			Unskilled			Farm operators		
	1948	1952	1954	1948	1952	1954	1948	1952	1954	1948	1952	1954	1948	1952	1954
Voted for:															
Democrat	15%	27%	22%	38%	28%	23%	52%	39%	26%	33%	40%	26%	25%	24%	22%
Republican	57	59	33	39	52	25	15	34	19	12	19	10	13	42	23
Other	1	2	--	*	1	--	1	1	--	*	1	--	2	1	--
Not ascertained	2	--	--	5	--	--	3	--	--	5	--	--	2	--	--
Did not vote	25	12	45	18	19	52	29	26	55	49	40	64	54	33	55
Not ascertained	--	--	--	--	--	--	--	--	--	1	--	--	4	--	--
	100%	100%	100%	100%	100%	100%	100%	100%	100%	100%	100%	100%	100%	100%	100%
Number of cases	117	333	246	79	155	102	164	462	337	85	174	144	105	178	104

Table III-11

RELATION OF LABOR UNION AFFILIATION
TO PROBABLE 1954 VOTE

| | Total population | | Skilled and unskilled laborers only | |
	Union member	Non-member	Union member	Non-member
Probable vote:				
Democratic	32%	21%	34%	17%
Republican	18	24	17	16
Probable non-voter	50	55	49	67
	100%	100%	100%	100%
Number of cases	316	808	240	235

When communities of different population density are compared (Table B-4), the tendency of union members to vote Democratic remains fairly constant regardless of community size, but metropolitan non-members were heavily Republican whereas rural non-members were, if anything, slightly Democratic. When income is controlled (Table B-5), union members at all income levels voted Democratic (the Democratic vote of union members in the $3000-6000 range was especially heavy), whereas non-members showed a slight Democratic majority when income was less than $3000 but shifted to an increasing Republican majority as income increased above the $3000 mark.

When education is controlled (as we noted on page 27), the Democratic majorities of union members remained practically the same regardless of educational attainment, whereas non-members voted Republican in increasing proportions as education increased. The union members of each educational level produced stronger Democratic majorities than was true of non-union persons at those educational levels.

When union membership among skilled and unskilled labor only is considered, the finding is that union labor voted heavily Democratic, whereas non-members of the same occupations were about evenly divided between the two parties. Another factor that stands out in the labor groups is that union membership is not only related to heavy Democratic majorities, but also to a considerably higher incidence of voting. Non-voting was much more common among non-union labor (see "Laborers only" columns of Table III-11).

When 1954 is compared with 1948 and 1952 in Table III-12 we note that in all three elections the total union vote was Democratic, whereas non-union voting was Republican. In 1948 especially, union members voted heavily Democratic. In all three elections a smaller proportion of union members compared with non-members failed to vote. It is interesting, however, that in the record turnout of 1952 the proportion of union members who voted increased only slightly—much less, for example, than that of professional and managerial people or farm operators.

Table III-12

RELATION OF LABOR UNION AFFILIATION TO VOTING BEHAVIOR IN THREE ELECTIONS

	Union member			Non-member		
	1948	1952	1954	1948	1952	1954
Voted for:						
Democrat	56%	43%	32%	25%	26%	21%
Republican	13	33	18	32	46	24
Other	1	1	--	2	1	--
Not ascertained	3	--	--	3	--	--
Did not vote	27	23	50	38	27	55
Not ascertained	--	--	--	*	--	--
	100%	100%	100%	100%	100%	100%
Number of cases	150	411	316	493	1165	808

Income

Table III-13 demonstrates a general tendency for persons with low incomes to vote Democratic in 1954 and those with high incomes to vote Republican. An exception to this rule is that persons with incomes less than $1000 gave a small majority to the Republicans. It should be noted that this income group is not made up exclusively of poor people in the usual sense of the word. It includes a certain number of retired people, widows, businessmen, farmers and others whose assets are substantial even though their income in any particular year may be very small. People with very high incomes (over $10,000) were

32

Table III-13

RELATION OF TOTAL FAMILY INCOME TO PROBABLE 1954 VOTE

	Under $1000	$1000-1999	$2000-2999	$3000-3999	$4000-4999	$5000-5999	$6000-7499	$7500-9999	$10,000 or more
Probable vote:									
Democratic	11%	25%	24%	25%	28%	28%	25%	23%	19%
Republican	14	15	19	19	23	21	29	30	46
Probable non-voter	75	60	57	56	49	51	46	47	35
	100%	100%	100%	100%	100%	100%	100%	100%	100%
Number of cases	96	129	142	194	150	145	100	66	74

by far the most one-sided of the income groups in their party choice, voting over two-to-one Republican.

Table III-14 presents the data for the 1948, 1952 and 1954 elections. In all three elections there is a tendency for lower-income groups to vote Democratic and upper-income groups to vote Republican. As one might expect, the income bracket at which votes are evenly divided between Republican and Democratic candidates is constantly moving up, reflecting the general rise in income levels. For the 1954 data the "over $5000" category is already unsatisfactory for finding the point of even vote division; Table III-13 shows this point to be found at approximately the $6000 level. Despite the shift in income distribution over these years, the relationship of party choice to relative position on the income scale remains about the same.

A final point to note in Table III-14 is that in all three elections compared, the higher the income level the higher the proportion of voters. Thus, although the persons in the lower brackets are more numerous and tend to vote Democratic, this fact is offset by the tendency of the higher-income voters, largely Republican, to go to the polls more faithfully.

Summary

A number of general observations may be drawn from the tables which have been presented in this chapter. To some extent the data merely document what has been known or presumed to be true on the basis of other kinds of information. The tables not only give precision to these commonplace generalities,

Table III-14

RELATION OF TOTAL FAMILY INCOME TO VOTING BEHAVIOR
IN THREE ELECTIONS

	Under $2000			$2000-2999			$3000-3999			$4000-4999			$5000 & over		
	1948	1952	1954	1948	1952	1954	1948	1952	1954	1948	1952	1954	1948	1952	1954
Voted for:															
Democrat	28%	23%	19%	37%	31%	24%	34%	35%	25%	34%	41%	28%	25%	28%	24%
Republican	16	30	14	17	36	19	34	40	19	37	41	23	53	59	30
Other	1	*	--	2	1	--	3	1	--	3	1	--	*	1	--
Not Ascertained	1	--	--	5	--	--	2	--	--	3	--	--	4	--	--
Did not vote	54	47	67	39	32	57	26	24	56	23	17	49	18	12	46
Not ascertained	--	--	--	--	--	--	1	--	--	--	--	--	--	--	--
	100%	100%	100%	100%	100%	100%	100%	100%	100%	100%	100%	100%	100%	100%	100%
Number of cases	178	315	225	185	255	142	142	364	194	65	233	150	84	415	385

however; they also make available information that would be very difficult to acquire through other channels.

Chapter III has been concerned with the phenomenon of group voting. Our data make it evident that a number of the major population categories have a persistent inclination toward one or the other of the two parties. The major theme of this group orientation in voting is social class. The prestige groups—educational, economic—are the most dependable sources of Republican support while the laborers, Negroes, unemployed, and other low-income and low-education groups are the strongest sources of the Democratic vote. There are also significant minor themes that do not appear to have a clear class-orientation. Jews, for example, are strong supporters of the Democratic party although they are not a disadvantaged social group.[1] Labor union membership adds a theme of a different kind, introducing an added group factor within the working-class population. The regional and nationality themes, although not considered in our analysis, provide additional dimensions of group voting.

Although group voting is clearly present in our data it should be remarked that the most partisan of the groups we have considered was far from unanimous in its voting choices. It may be that in local situations, such as a precinct of New York City, a particular segment of the electorate might line up *en masse* behind one or the other parties. This does not happen on the national scale, however, as it apparently does in some European countries.[2] Thus the labor leader who exhorts the national membership to turn out in behalf of the Democratic party must face the prospect that a third or more of those who vote will support the Republican candidate. None of the major population groups we have considered is fully committed to either party.

The ability of these groups to break out of their established vote patterns under the stress of unusual circumstances is amply demonstrated in the 1952 data. The Korean war and the appeal of a personable and widely admired candidate introduced powerful new forces on the voters and resulted in a realignment of many of the groups we have been considering. Although the

---

1. See Fuchs, L. H. for a recent discussion of the Jewish vote, "American Jews and the Presidential Vote, " *American Political Science Review*, June 1955.

2. Rokkan, S. , *Party Identification and Opinions on Issues on Domestic and International Policy* (mimeographed), 1955.

groups which had been most strongly Republican or Democratic in 1948 still held those positions in 1952, the absolute values of their votes for the two parties changed greatly. The 1952 experience is a convincing demonstration of the hazards of attempting to explain the vote solely on the basis of group membership.

The fact that labor union members, Catholics, college people, Negroes and the other groups we have examined differ substantially and consistently in the support they give the two major parties need not lead us into over-simplifications regarding the motivation of their votes. It is not necessary to assume, for example, because Catholics are more likely to vote Democratic than Republican that Catholics as individuals are conforming to a strong political group standard which is forced on them by their fellow religionists.

An alternative explanation might propose that Catholics vote Democratic because at the time of the Irish, Polish, and Italian migrations to this country these groups were captured by the Democratic party in the eastern metropolises. As they developed into good Americans they also developed into good Democrats. They passed their new nationality and their party identification on to their children. Their descendants are still voting Democratic, not because they are Catholics but because they are Democrats.

We have also assumed that a strong political majority may develop within a population group entirely on the basis of independent decisions by individual members of that group. If external circumstances affect a large proportion of the members of some large group in a similar way there is likely to be considerable similarity in their response; yet the individual members may not be aware of any group standard or indeed even know of the reaction of the other members. One may speculate, for example, as to the development of the Democratic vote among Negroes. Litchfield's study in Detroit[1] demonstrates that this was entirely a phenomenon of the Roosevelt era. Some individual Negroes must have come to the conclusion from watching the New Deal and the Roosevelt family that the Democratic party held more promise for them than did the Republican. As they shifted to the Democratic party they moved against the traditional Negro attachment to "the party of Lincoln." It is conceivable that a large part of the developing Democratic

---

1. Litchfield, E. H. , *Voting Behavior in a Metropolitan Area* in Michigan Governmental Studies, No. 7, 1941, iii-93.

majority among Negroes resulted from this kind of individual decision although it is likely that as the movement grew group effects on individual Negroes also became important.

The most interesting example of group differences to be found in our study, however, does not come from consideration of these demographic variables but from a political variable, party identification. We can make a much better prediction of how a man thinks and acts politically if we know whether he calls himself a Republican or a Democrat than if we know he calls himself a skilled worker, a Catholic, a suburbanite, a rich man, or a pauper. We consider this factor of party identification and its relation to the 1954 vote in Chapter IV.

IV

THE VOTES OF THE
PARTY IDENTIFICATION GROUPS

The population groups which we have considered in Chapter III are all familiar categories in political analysis. The fact that a great many Americans call themselves Republicans or Democrats is also a commonplace observation but it is an aspect of political life that until recently has been quite inadequately dealt with in studies of political behavior.

In introducing this discussion of the 1954 votes of the party identification groups it is necessary to emphasize the distinction we are making between party identifiers and voters. Although the terms "Republicans" or "Democrats" are often used in common parlance to refer to the people who intend to vote or have voted for the candidate of one or the other party, they are used here to refer to the individual's self-identification as a "Republican" or "Democrat." We regard this party attachment as one of the factors that influence attitudes and votes but, as we saw in our 1952 study, it is by no means the only factor. A person whom we classify as a Republican may or may not vote; he may vote for either party.

The 1954 votes of the party identification groups are shown in Table IV-1. It is not surprising to find that within each party group those people who voted tended strongly to support the candidate of the party with which they identified. Among these voters, however, weak Republicans voted Republican approximately as heavily as did strong Republicans, while weak Democrats crossed party lines to vote Republican far more frequently than did strong Democrats. Thus, the potential Democratic vote majority that would have occurred in 1954 if party identification had been the only determinant of vote was not realized, in part because many more Democrats than Republicans voted for candidates of the opposite party.

38

Table IV-1 also makes clear another reason for the reduction of the large potential Democratic vote of 1954 to a small actual majority. Among the population at large, greater proportions of Democrats than Republicans failed to vote at all; the percentages of non-voting strong and weak Democrats are greater than the respective percentages for strong and weak Republicans. Because of the relatively high failure of Democrats to cast ballots, the election was much closer than would have been predicted from a knowledge of the distribution of party affiliations alone.

Table IV-1

RELATION OF PARTY IDENTIFICATION TO 1952 VOTE AND PROBABLE 1954 VOTE

	Strong Democrat		Weak Democrat		Independent Democrat		Independent		Independent Republican		Weak Republican		Strong Republican	
	1952	1954	1952	1954	1952	1954	1952	1954	1952	1954	1952	1954	1952	1954
Vote:														
Democratic	63%	57%	42%	30%	44%	25%	14%	10%	5%	3%	5%	3%	1%	4%
Republican	12	1	26	10	28	11	57	12	73	40	73	45	91	69
Other	1	--	1	--	2	--	3	--	--	--	--	--	--	--
Probable non-voter	24	42	31	60	26	64	26	78	22	57	22	52	8	27
	100%	100%	100%	100%	100%	100%	100%	100%	100%	100%	100%	100%	100%	100%
Number of cases	351	248	402	288	164	97	87	82	114	68	222	159	217	146

Table IV-1 also presents the presidential votes of the different party identification groups in 1952. Comparison of the 1952 and 1954 data makes possible a rough estimation of the relative importance of party identification in the two elections. It is clear that Republican party identifiers showed very little inclination to cross party lines in either of the votes. Democratic identifiers on the other hand left their party in favor of Eisenhower in 1952 in much greater numbers than they deserted their congressional candidates in 1954. It cannot be concluded from this fact that congressional votes are always more party-line than presidential votes. The 1948 presidential vote appears to have been highly party-determined. The data do indicate, however, that the candidate and issue factors which were instrumental in creating Democratic defections in 1952, although still present to a visible degree, were less effective in the 1954 election.

In this chapter the party identification of the major population categories will be presented and the voting records of these different groups of party identifiers will be examined. This will tell us whether the party crossing and the non-voting observed in Table IV-1 are general throughout the population or concentrated in certain special groups. It will also provide the basis of a subsequent analysis of the relative importance of the various types of group membership we are considering in the determination of political acts and attitudes.

Men and Women

Table IV-2 presents the party identification of men and women as of October 1954. The members of both sexes identified more frequently with the Democratic party than with the Republican, men in slightly greater proportions than women. Thus, both categories are Democratic in identification. It will be remembered, however, that women voted narrowly Republican in 1954 while men were clearly Democratic (Table III-1).

Table IV-2

PARTY IDENTIFICATION OF MEN AND WOMEN

Party identification	Men	Women
Strong Democrat	25%	20%
Weak Democrat	25	25
Independent Democrat	10	7
Independent	7	7
Independent Republican	6	6
Weak Republican	13	15
Strong Republican	12	14
Apolitical, don't know	2	6
	100%	100%
Number of cases	532	607

Table IV-3 presents simultaneous data on sex, party identification, and voting behavior. This table shows us that vote defections of women were, if anything, less frequent than those of men. The differences are very small but they are in the same direction for both Democratic and Republican identifiers. In 1954 at least, women who voted appear to have been more securely held by the factor of party loyalty than were men.

The table also shows that for both sexes there was a greater incidence of non-voting among strong Democrats than among strong Republicans, and among weak Democrats than among weak Republicans. Non-voting among women was more frequent proportionately than among men for each of the corresponding party identifications, but Democratic women in particular stayed away from the polls. The data make it clear that Republican women gave greater support to the party of their choice than did Democratic women.

Table IV-3

RELATION OF PARTY IDENTIFICATION TO PROBABLE
1954 CONGRESSIONAL VOTE AMONG MEN AND WOMEN

	Men					Women				
	SD[1]	WD	Ind	WR	SR	SD	WD	Ind	WR	SR
Probable vote:										
Democratic	64%	35%	15%	6%	8%	50%	25%	12%	1%	1%
Republican	2	14	21	47	67	1	7	18	43	71
Probable non-voter	34	51	64	47	25	49	68	70	56	28
	100%	100%	100%	100%	100%	100%	100%	100%	100%	100%
Number of cases	130	132	123	68	64	117	154	123	91	82

The source of this discrepancy in turnout becomes apparent if we keep in mind the demographic location of the Democratic and Republican strength. As we shall see, Republicans are most numerous among the high-income, high-education, high-occupational status groups. Democrats are most frequent in the contrasting categories. Because of their greater emancipation from the cultural stereotype of the non-political woman, women in the higher status categories are more likely to vote than are women of the less favored categories. For example, if we compare the voting of men and women of the grade school and college-educated groups we find the following:

---

1. In this and some subsequent tables the names of the party groups are abbreviated in order to save space, i.e., for SD read Strong Democrats, etc.

	Voted in 1954	Did not vote
Grade school only:		
Men	45%	55
Women	32%	68
College:		
Men	60%	40
Women	59%	41

We see that women at the higher educational level were as likely to vote as the corresponding men but at the grade school level women were clearly deficient. If this discrepancy were wiped out the Democratic party undoubtedly would benefit.

Age

The relationship between age and party identification is presented in Table IV-4. The tendency to identify with a party apparently increases to some extent with advance in age; 80 percent of our respondents over 65 called themselves strong or weak members of one of the two major parties. The ratio of

Table IV-4

RELATION OF AGE TO PARTY IDENTIFICATION

Party identification	21-24	25-34	35-44	45-54	55-64	Over 65
Strong Democrat	14%	25%	19%	20%	25%	23%
Weak Democrat	27	29	26	23	28	19
Independent Democrat	12	9	10	8	7	7
Independent	9	7	7	8	7	7
Independent Republican	11	5	7	7	6	1
Weak Republican	11	12	14	16	10	19
Strong Republican	8	9	11	16	16	19
Apolitical, don't know	8	4	6	2	1	5
	100%	100%	100%	100%	100%	100%
Number of cases	74	292	247	238	135	146

42

strong to weak partisans also increases in the higher age groups. Advancing maturity appears to be associated with increasingly clear perception of one's own political partisanship.

At each age level more respondents claimed Democratic than Republican identification. In general, respondents under 45 years of age more frequently identified with the Democrats than was true of respondents over 45. Our data are not adequate to answer the question of whether this age shift reflects a long-term aging process in the Republican party or a tendency of young Democrats to turn to the Republican party in their later years.

It will be remembered that voters over 45 years of age voted Republican in 1954 whereas voters under 45 gave the Democrats a majority (Table III-3). Table IV-5 compares the votes of party identification groups within the younger and older age brackets. The data show that people over 45 were similar to people under 45 in one respect: Strong and weak Democrats were less likely to vote than strong and weak Republicans at both age levels. While the turnout of Democrats over 45 was only slightly greater than that of Democrats under 45, the voting record of the older Republicans was significantly better than that of the younger Republicans, especially among the strongly identified. Party switching was not markedly different in the two age brackets; weak Democrats being the most frequent defectors at both age levels.

Table IV-5

RELATION OF PARTY IDENTIFICATION TO PROBABLE
CONGRESSIONAL VOTE AMONG AGE GROUPS

	Under 45 years					Over 45 years				
	SD	WD	Ind	WR	SR	SD	WD	Ind	WR	SR
Probable vote:										
Democratic	55%	30%	13%	4%	2%	60%	30%	16%	3%	6%
Republican	2	8	15	40	60	1	13	25	50	74
Probable non-voter	43	62	72	56	38	39	57	59	47	20
	100%	100%	100%	100%	100%	100%	100%	100%	100%	100%
Number of cases	132	168	144	78	58	115	119	101	79	87

Religion

Table IV-6 shows the party identification of the major religious groups. Jews, Catholics, and Protestants, in that order, identify more heavily with the Democratic than the Republican party. ·

Table IV-6

RELATION OF RELIGION TO PARTY IDENTIFICATION

Party identification	Protestant	Catholic	Jewish
Strong Democrat	21%	23%	21%
Weak Democrat	25	27	32
Independent Democrat	7	13	18
Independent	7	7	6
Independent Republican	6	5	6
Weak Republican	15	12	8
Strong Republican	15	8	6
Apolitical, don't know	4	5	3
	100%	100%	100%
Number of cases	857	216	34

The Protestant vote was evenly split in 1954 (Table III-4) despite the heavy Democratic identification shown in Table IV-6, whereas both Catholic and Jewish vote and identification were Democratic. Table IV-7 shows the 1954 vote of the variously identified people within each religious group. (Jews are omitted from Table IV-7 because their numbers are too small to permit further division.) There was no clear difference between Protestant and Catholic voters in their tendency to cross party lines. There was a substantial difference, however, in the turnout of Protestants and Catholics of similar party identification. In every category the Catholics were more likely to have voted. As we have seen earlier this fact very probably derives less from considerations of religious group membership than it does from the historical accident that American Catholics are for the most part a Northern, white, metropolitan group.

Table IV-7

RELATION OF PARTY IDENTIFICATION TO PROBABLE CONGRESSIONAL VOTE AMONG RELIGIOUS GROUPS

	Protestants					Catholics				
	SD	WD	Ind	WR	SR	SD	WD	Ind	WR	SR
Probable vote:										
Democratic	54%	26%	13%	4%	2%	65%	45%	18%	--%	--%
Republican	1	8	20	40	68	2	19	18	60	--
Probable non-voter	45	66	67	56	30	33	36	64	40	--
	100%	100%	100%	100%	100%	100%	100%	100%	100%	100%
Number of cases	184	213	173	128	123	51	58	55	25	18

Race

Table IV-8 compares the distributions of party identification of the two major races. The Negro population, once regarded as adhering to the Republican party, is now clearly attached to the opposite camp. Sixteen percent of the Negroes reported that they were either "apolitical" or "didn't know" to which party they belonged.

Table IV-8

RELATION OF RACE TO PARTY IDENTIFICATION

Party identification	White	Negro
Strong Democrat	22%	23%
Weak Democrat	25	28
Independent Democrat	9	6
Independent	7	5
Independent Republican	6	6
Weak Republican	15	5
Strong Republican	13	11
Apolitical, don't know	3	16
	100%	100%
Number of cases	1022	103

The number of Negro voters in our sample is too small to permit racial, party identification, and voting comparisons of any consequence.

Type of Community

The most interesting difference in the party identification of people living in communities of different population density is that found between the metropolitan centers and their suburbs (Table IV-9). The metropolitan centers which have long been regarded as the core of Democratic strength have in fact the greatest disproportion of self-styled Democrats over Republicans. The autonomous political character of the suburbs appears when we discover that in these areas two-thirds of the people who call themselves Republicans say they are "strong" Republicans while two-thirds of the Democrats say they are "weak" Democrats. This is a clear contrast to the other types of community. The metropolitan suburbs are the only area in which strong Republicans outnumber strong Democrats.

These data raise questions of both practical and theoretical interest. As we have stated earlier, we do not know whether the greater Republican strength in the suburbs results from the

Table IV-9

RELATION OF TYPE OF COMMUNITY
TO PARTY IDENTIFICATION

Party identification	Metro-politan centers	Metro-politan suburbs	City or town	Open country
Strong Democrat	22%	15%	22%	25%
Weak Democrat	27	32	25	21
Independent Democrat	11	9	7	10
Independent	7	5	8	7
Independent Republican	5	9	7	3
Weak Republican	11	9	15	18
Strong Republican	12	20	12	10
Apolitical, don't know	5	1	4	6
	100%	100%	100%	100%
Number of cases	169	150	601	219

Table IV-10

RELATION OF PARTY IDENTIFICATION TO PROBABLE 1954 CONGRESSIONAL VOTE WITHIN TYPE OF COMMUNITY

	Metropolitan centers					Metropolitan suburbs					City or town					Open country				
	SD	WD	Ind	WR	SR	SD	WD	Ind	WR	SR	SD	WD	Ind	WR	SR	SD	WD	Ind	WR	SR
Probable vote:																				
Democratic	59%	33%	18%	--%	--%	55%	25%	24%	--%	3%	62%	32%	11%	4%	6%	44%	26%	9%	5%	5%
Republican	--	7	18	--	71	--	6	29	--	80	2	14	20	44	67	2	2	12	33	59
Probable non-voter	41	60	64	--	29	45	69	47	--	17	36	54	69	52	27	54	72	79	62	36
	100%	100%	100%	100%	100%	100%	100%	100%	100%	100%	100%	100%	100%	100%	100%	100%	100%	100%	100%	100%
Number of cases	37	45	38	18	21	22	48	34	13	30	134	149	132	88	73	55	46	43	40	22

47

in-migration of people of Republican inclination or from the influence of Republican community standards on the in-migrants after they arrive. It would be of great interest to know whether the large proportion of weak Democrats we see in the suburban column of Table IV-9 are relatively recent arrivals whose attachment to the Democratic party is fading and who are on their way to becoming Republicans.

One piece of evidence which suggests that this may not be the case is seen in Table IV-10 where we find that Democrats, both strong and weak, were about as likely to vote for their own party's candidates in the suburbs as they were in the metropolitan centers. If their party loyalty was under serious pressure from a Republican atmosphere in these suburban communities we should expect to find them crossing party lines in their votes more commonly than their Democratic fellows in the metropolitan centers.

Although the columns in Table IV-10 are based on very small numbers of cases there is some suggestion that the greatest Democratic defections were not in the metropolitan areas but in the smaller cities and towns. In contrast Democrats in the open country were least likely to abandon their party's candidate, a very interesting change from 1952 when this group broke heavily to the Eisenhower ticket.

As we have seen in the earlier tables the Republican party's greatest advantage in 1954 was not its gains from Democratic defectors but the fact that its followers went to the polls and voted in greater proportion than did the Democrats. A close examination of Table IV-10 will show that every comparison of Republican and Democratic party identifiers, strong or weak, in all four types of community, reveals this discrepancy in turnout. Although the Republican party is a minority party in terms of the labels people attach to themselves, it appears to make more effective use of its strength than does the Democratic opposition.

Education

As Table IV-11 makes clear, party identification differs substantially among people of different educational levels. Republican identification increases progressively as years of formal education increase. When intensity of identification is considered, moreover, the proportion of Democratic identifiers who call themselves "strong Democrats" declines as educational level increases. Among the college-educated the numbers of Democrats

48

Table IV-11

RELATION OF EDUCATION TO PARTY IDENTIFICATION

Party identification	Grade school	High school	College
Strong Democrat	26%	21%	13%
Weak Democrat	25	27	22
Independent Democrat	6	9	11
Independent	8	7	7
Independent Republican	3	7	11
Weak Republican	13	14	17
Strong Republican	10	13	18
Apolitical, don't know	9	2	1
	100%	100%	100%
Number of cases	416	517	202

and Republicans are equal, but half of the Republicans are strong identifiers while only one third of the Democrats are.

Table IV-12 shows the vote of party identifiers of different educational levels. We see that the Democratic failure to turn out in proportions equal to their Republican counterparts is heaviest at the lower educational levels. The discrepancy in the turnout of the party adherents decreases as education increases; among the college-educated the data are thin and the picture is ambiguous. It is perhaps safest to say that if there is a party difference in turnout at this level it is less than at the lower levels.

On the other hand, willingness to cross party lines does not seem to be more characteristic of one educational level than another. Among Democrats, the number of defectors was larger in the high school and college groups but of those who voted the proportions who voted for the Republican candidates did not differ greatly at the three educational levels. Among Republicans there was relatively little defection at any level but, if anything, college people were least likely to support an opposition candidate.

The attitudes of people of much and little formal education toward party regularity are more complex than these data would indicate. We know, for example, from our two previous election studies that people of high education are more likely to

49

Table IV-12

RELATION OF PARTY IDENTIFICATION TO PROBABLE 1954 CONGRESSIONAL VOTE AMONG EDUCATIONAL GROUPS

	Grade school					High school					College				
	SD	WD	Ind	WR	SR	SD	WD	Ind	WR	SR	SD	WD	Ind	WR	SR
Probable vote:															
Democratic	52%	24%	12%	--%	7%	59%	28%	14%	7%	3%	69%	49%	15%	--%	3%
Republican	1	6	16	39	63	2	10	18	46	67	--	18	27	50	80
Probable non-voter	47	70	72	61	30	39	62	68	47	30	31	33	58	50	17
	100%	100%	100%	100%	100%	100%	100%	100%	100%	100%	100%	100%	100%	100%	100%
Number of cases	110	102	69	54	43	111	139	118	71	67	26	45	59	34	36

Table IV-13

RELATION OF OCCUPATION OF FAMILY HEAD TO PARTY IDENTIFICATION

Party identification	Professional, technical	Business, managerial	Clerical	Sales	Skilled labor	Un-skilled labor	Farm	Retired	Un-employed
Strong Democrat	13%	13%	16%	14%	26%	25%	24%	24%	31%
Weak Democrat	25	31	22	20	25	29	21	18	21
Independent Democrat	7	9	10	9	11	6	8	7	12
Independent	9	8	2	7	7	7	5	7	12
Independent Republican	17	8	16	18	2	6	3	3	--
Weak Republican	16	15	19	14	15	6	16	15	12
Strong Republican	13	14	14	18	9	10	19	25	3
Apolitical, don't know	--	2	1	--	5	11	4	1	9
	100%	100%	100%	100%	100%	100%	100%	100%	100%
Number of cases	84	162	58	44	337	144	104	100	33

split their tickets in presidential elections than are less well educated people.[1] They are a little more likely to call themselves Independents but no less likely to call themselves "strong" adherents if they do associate themselves with a party label (Table IV-11). The influence of formal education on one's concept of his political role is an important problem but beyond the scope of our present study.

Occupation of Family Head

The so-called "business community" in the United States is often regarded as the stronghold of the Republican party. One of the most familiar criticisms made by Democrats of the Republican party is that it is the party of businessmen. As we saw in Chapter III the business and managerial group gave the Republican candidates for Congress a sizable majority of their votes in the 1954 election. And yet, when we ask these people whether they "think of themselves" as Republicans or Democrats, more say Democrat than Republican (Table IV-13). To be sure, most of the Democrats call themselves "weak" Democrats but they clearly out-number the strong and weak Republicans.

The answer to the discrepancy between identification and votes in this group is seen in Table IV-14. (Because of the small size of the various occupational categories, several of them have been combined or omitted from this table.) In the combined professional-technical-business-managerial category, strong and weak Democrats did not vote as heavily as did strong and weak Republicans, respectively, and those Democrats who did vote were more likely to cross party lines than were Republican voters. The result was a heavy Republican vote from a category that reports more Democratic identifiers than Republican.

It is not surprising to find that skilled and unskilled labor are the most Democratic of the occupational groups in their party affiliations. These are large groups numerically and even though their vote was not near their potential it is obvious that they made a substantial contribution to the Democratic cause in 1954. Farmers, who are often spoken of as solidly Republican, are in fact divided, with a high proportion of strong partisans at both extremes. A sizable number of them, it must be remembered, are located in the rural and Democratic South.

---

1. See *The Voter Decides*, page 96.

52

It is perplexing to find in Table IV-14 that skilled workers of Democratic persuasion show the same failure to vote and tendency to defect that we observed among the business and professional Democrats. We might have been inclined to identify these aspects of the voting of the business and professional Democrats as reactions to pressure from the Republican atmosphere generally thought to characterize business circles. This might appear to be an example of "conforming to group standards." But this explanation will not fit the Democratic skilled workers, who, if group standards were effective, should be more solid in support of their party than the greatly outnumbered Republicans in this occupational group. Instead they are less solid, and so far as these data go we can come to no clear decision regarding the influence of the political norms of occupational groups on individual members of these groups.

Table IV-14

RELATION OF PARTY IDENTIFICATION TO PROBABLE 1954
CONGRESSIONAL VOTE AMONG OCCUPATIONAL GROUPS

	Professional-business					Skilled workers				
	SD	WD	Ind	WR	SR	SD	WD	Ind	WR	SR
Probable vote:										
Democratic	53%	35%	15%	--%	6%	64%	23%	13%	--%	3%
Republican	6	17	26	62	76	--	12	15	40	80
Probable non-voter	41	48	59	38	18	36	65	72	60	17
	100%	100%	100%	100%	100%	100%	100%	100%	100%	100%
Number of cases	32	72	69	37	33	89	84	69	48	30

Labor Union Affiliation

As we have seen in Table III-12, union members gave the Democratic party a two-to-one majority in their 1954 votes. Their party identification, as we see in Table IV-15, is even more heavily Democratic.

Most union members are found in the skilled and unskilled worker categories. If we compare these union members to the people in these occupations who are not union members we have the clearest demonstration of the relationship between union membership and political behavior (Table IV-17). Union labor is clearly more closely associated with the Democratic party than is non-union labor although the latter group is more Democratic in its orientation than is the non-union public at large (Table IV-16). In voting union labor has a higher turnout and there is some indication that this is especially true of those of Democratic identification.

Table IV-15

RELATION OF LABOR UNION AFFILIATION
TO PARTY IDENTIFICATION

Party identification	Total population		Laborers only	
	Union member	Non-member	Union member	Non-member
Strong Democrat	27%	20%	29%	22%
Weak Democrat	30	24	32	21
Independent Democrat	10	8	8	11
Independent	6	7	6	9
Independent Republican	4	7	2	4
Weak Republican	11	15	11	13
Strong Republican	9	14	8	10
Apolitical, don't know	3	5	4	10
	100%	100%	100%	100%
Number of cases	315	808	240	235

Although union labor is the most highly Democratic of all the population categories we have examined, there is no evidence in our data that this fact has the slightest influence on the voting of those union workers who identify with the Republican party. It may be that, over time, people in the union-worker group tend to move over into the Democratic camp, but those who called themselves Republicans in our 1954 survey showed no sign of weakening in their party loyalty. Union membership may have had the effect of making Democratic identifiers more solid in the support of their party, but the ability of Republican workers to resist this pressure is impressive.

Table IV-16

RELATION OF PARTY IDENTIFICATION TO PROBABLE
1954 CONGRESSIONAL VOTE AMONG UNION
AND NON-UNION GROUPS

	Total sample									
	Union member					Non-member				
	SD	WD	Ind	WR	SR	SD	WD	Ind	WR	SR
Probable vote:										
Democratic	69%	32%	18%	3%	3%	51%	29%	12%	3%	4%
Republican	--	9	16	40	79	2	10	21	46	67
Probable non-voter	31	59	66	57	18	47	61	67	51	29
	100%	100%	100%	100%	100%	100%	100%	100%	100%	100%
Number of cases	86	95	62	35	29	158	190	182	123	116

Table IV-17

RELATION OF PARTY IDENTIFICATION TO PROBABLE
1954 CONGRESSIONAL VOTE AMONG UNION
AND NON-UNION LABOR

	Skilled and unskilled workers only									
	Union member					Non-member				
	SD	WD	Ind	WR	SR	SD	WD	Ind	WR	SR
Probable vote:										
Democratic	73%	29%	20%	4%	--%	52%	16%	7%	3%	4%
Republican	--	10	18	35	85	--	8	11	39	63
Probable non-voter	27	61	62	61	15	48	76	82	58	33
	100%	100%	100%	100%	100%	100%	100%	100%	100%	100%
Number of cases	70	76	39	26	20	52	49	56	31	24

Income

Party identification does not appear to vary greatly by income class, except at the high and low extremes of the income scale (Table IV-18). The small proportion of the population whose incomes run over $10,000 a year are heavily committed to the Republican party, not only in the proportion who identify themselves as Republicans but in the strength of this identification as well. At the low end of the income ladder the peculiarly heterogeneous group with incomes of less than $1,000 has a high proportion of strong Democrats but also has a sizable proportion of strong Republicans.

Table IV-18

RELATION OF TOTAL FAMILY INCOME TO PARTY IDENTIFICATION

Party identification	Under $1000	$1000-1999	$2000-2999	$3000-3999	$4000-4999	$5000-5999	$6000-7499	$7500-9999	Over $10,000
Strong Democrat	32%	23%	24%	23%	21%	20%	22%	17%	7%
Weak Democrat	15	32	22	25	30	28	30	24	14
Independent Democrat	7	6	8	7	9	13	5	12	11
Independent	6	8	11	7	7	6	8	6	5
Independent Republican	--	5	5	6	8	4	9	8	12
Weak Republican	6	12	11	17	15	16	18	9	22
Strong Republican	18	8	13	12	7	12	7	20	28
Apolitical, don't know	16	6	6	3	3	1	1	4	1
	100%	100%	100%	100%	100%	100%	100%	100%	100%
Number of cases	96	129	142	194	150	145	100	66	74

Recent shifts in the income levels of different occupations make it more difficult to interpret income as a sociological variable than might have been the case ten years ago. Many factory workers now have incomes in the $4,000 to $6,000 class and if their wives are working the family income will be considerably higher. In the meantime income raises for some white-collar groups have not been nearly as large. As a consequence, except at the highest income levels, the relationships

Table IV-19

RELATION OF PARTY IDENTIFICATION TO PROBABLE CONGRESSIONAL VOTE AMONG INCOME GROUPS

	Under $3000					$3000 - 6000					Over $6000				
	SD	WD	Ind	WR	SR	SD	WD	Ind	WR	SR	SD	WD	Ind	WR	SR
Probable vote:															
Democratic	46%	29%	11%	--%	2%	62%	31%	17%	5%	6%	66%	32%	13%	2%	5%
Republican	1	4	14	43	62	1	11	18	39	73	--	18	29	63	76
Probable non-voter	53	67	75	57	36	37	58	65	56	21	34	50	58	35	19
	100%	100%	100%	100%	100%	100%	100%	100%	100%	100%	100%	100%	100%	100%	100%
Number of cases	94	86	71	37	47	105	134	107	78	52	38	56	60	40	41

which used to exist between income, occupation and education have been considerably altered. Knowing a man's income doesn't tell us as much about him as it once did.

The substantial commitment to the Republican party of people of more than $10,000 income is a matter of more than casual interest. Although this group numbers less than ten percent of the population, it is obvious that its prominence and influence in American society must be far greater than this small proportion would indicate. It seems a safe assumption that, granting some occupational exceptions such as ministers and teachers, most of the people holding prominent positions of leadership, authority, and prestige in this country fall in this income class. As our data show, strong Republicans outnumber strong Democrats at this income level by a margin of four to one.

The political implications of these facts may be considerable. If high-status people are publicly seen as predominantly Republican, does this tend to give a class flavor to the two-party system in the United States, especially when contrasted to the strong Democratic orientation of the low-income, laboring group? If Republican party membership is widely seen as a mark of high social status, does this tend to move upward-mobile people toward the Republican party as their social aspiration level rises? Are estimates of "public opinion" on political issues, based on public statements, newspaper editorials, letters to congressmen and the like, subject to a persistent Republican bias because they come disproportionately from this high-status level of society? Our present data do not give us the answers to these questions.

Combining the income classes into three categories, as is done in Table IV-19, obscures the differences between the smaller groups. However, it makes it possible to see the voting records of Democrats and Republicans at different income levels. Two facts merit comment: Republicans turned out in greater numbers than Democrats at all three income levels and the defections among the weak Democrats seemed correlated with income, the group over $6,000 having the largest proportion voting Republican.

The Democratic deficiencies in turnout are now a familiar theme in this report; this is the first table, however, which has shown a consistent relationship with Democratic defections. Strong Democrats in the higher-income bracket were considerably more likely to cross party lines than were those at lower-income levels. We may surmise that these high income Democrats were in conflict for either or both of two reasons: As we have suggested, they may have been reacting to the Republican norm of high income people. In view of their better-than-average incomes they may also have found attractive Republican party policies on taxation and spending. The force of these considerations, or others less obvious, apparently overcame whatever sense of loyalty these weak identifiers felt toward their party.

Summary.

As we have stated earlier, it is our belief that one of the major forces that motivates the individual citizen in his political behavior is his sense of identification with a political party. There are no doubt many factors which must be taken into account if we hope to understand fully the vagaries of the vote. Our data lead us to conclude that party identification is one of the most important among them.

We have used a very simple measure of party identification, asking the respondent to classify himself according to what he "usually thought" himself to be. This classification, when expanded by a statement of intensity (strong or weak), is more highly correlated with the 1954 vote than any of the other population variables shown in Chapter III. Strong party identifiers in particular are the most likely to vote and the most likely to support their own party.

The influence of factors other than party identification is particularly clear in respect to turnout. In many of the tables of Chapter IV the choice of candidates by party groups is very consistent from one population bracket to another but the total turnout varies substantially between brackets. The different educational groups, for example, differ a good deal in the proportions who were classified as probable voters but the strong Democrats who were so classified gave the Democratic party virtually 100 percent of their vote no matter what educational level they were in. Other identification categories were equally consistent. Party identification apparently has a greater effect on how a person would vote if he voted than on whether he actually gets to the polls or not. This supports the findings of our 1952 study from which we concluded, "It may be that for many people party identification does not have the capacity to stimulate overt activity, but does have the power to command support on the psychological level of preferences and attitudes."

Chapter IV leaves us with two important and difficult questions: Why did Republicans turn out in larger proportions than Democrats in virtually every population category we have examined? and, Why did Democrats defect in greater numbers than Republicans?

The relatively poor turnout of people who call themselves Democrats was not unique to the 1954 election. We recorded the same phenomenon in our study of the 1952 election. The detailed tables of the present report permit us to evaluate the commonly heard hypothesis that the low Democratic turnout in national elections results from the fact that Democrats come disproportionately from the less politicized strata of society. This now appears to be only a partial explanation since we find that Democrats at all status levels have a poorer voting record than their Republican counterparts.

It will occur to the reader that the Democratic record reflects the heavy contribution that the South makes to the Democratic ranks. Since turnout in the South is lower than in the rest of the nation it might be expected that national data on Democratic turnout would be lower than national Republican figures. However, it will be remembered that our metropolitan data, which are exclusively Northern, showed the same Democratic deficiencies that appear in the other tables. Moreover, removing the South from the other tables does not alter the picture greatly; Republicans still have better voting records than Democrats.

There are a number of additional hypotheses that might be advanced to explain these data. Is it possible, for example, that Republican party followers are subjected to greater pressure through the mass media than Democrats and thus are more highly motivated to vote? Is the Republican party organization more effective in canvassing its membership and getting it to the polls? Is our measure of party identification too crude—are Republicans actually more firmly attached to their party than Democrats to theirs? Does the Republican party tend to attract a different kind of "personality" than is typically found in the Democratic party?[1]

---

1. Differences between Republicans and Democrats on items from the California F scale are reported at all three educational levels by Lane, R. E., "Political Personality and Electoral Choice," *American Political Science Review, 49*, No. 1, 1955, 173-190.

None of these suggestions can be evaluated on the basis of our present study. None of them may be the correct explanation of the mysterious Democratic deficit at the polls.

The Democratic defections which we have seen in the tables of this chapter might be thought of in two ways—either as a reaction to the specific circumstances of the 1954 election or as an expression of a long term trend away from the Democrats. The data seem to favor the first of these explanations.

Although we do not have data regarding party identification prior to 1952, we know that that election was won by the Republicans largely as the result of large-scale desertions among the Democrats. It was our conclusion in our earlier report that this was brought about primarily by a combination of anxiety regarding the international situation and a perception of Mr. Eisenhower as a man uniquely capable of handling this situation. The 1954 defections were not as great as those in 1952 but it would appear that, even though the Korean war was no longer an issue in 1954, the presence of Mr. Eisenhower as head of the Republican party was still an influential force in that election.

The alternative explanation of the Democratic defections is not completely without merit. Party crossing among people who admit their party connection is "weak" could reasonably be thought of as a preliminary step to actual conversion from one party to the other. There is the additional relevant fact that in 1952 we found more Republicans who said they had once been Democrats than Democrats who would admit ever having been Republicans. This would indicate a gradual slippage of Democrats into the Republican ranks. The stubborn fact which confounds this theory, however, is the total absence of change in the distributions of party identifiers between 1952 and 1954. If a slow-moving trend toward the Republican party is going on there should be not only defections but conversions, and these we do not find.

We turn now in Chapter V from voting to attitudes on political issues. We have seen how the important population categories turned out and cast their ballots; we will now see how these different kinds of people reacted to some of the major political questions which were prominent during the 1954 campaign.

V

THE ATTITUDES OF THE POPULATION GROUPS

The study of issues elaborates our picture of the political characteristics of the population groups with which we are concerned and permits the examination of questions which cannot be answered by the study of the vote alone. We will be interested in this chapter not only in the group reactions to the specific questions presented but also in the patterning of attitudes which different groups may show and in the question of whether these attitudes result from influences external to the group itself or from what we have called "group effects."

In order to compare the views of the various population groups on the eight questions regarding issues which were asked in our interview it is necessary to review a large number of tables. We will attempt to simplify this presentation by considering each question in order and discussing the responses given to it by each of the several groups. The tables themselves are presented in the Appendix.

The Performance of the Republican Party

As we saw in Chapter II, the first two questions in our series on political issues concerned the performance of the Republican administration. The respondents were asked what in their opinion were the "best thing" and the "worst thing" the Republican party had done in its two years in office. It will be noted that these were open-ended questions; that is, no prearranged categories were presented for the respondent's choice. The interviewer simply wrote down what the respondent said. Although a large number of different answers were given to these two questions, most of them could be subsumed under a limited number of categories. Tables B-6 to B-14 show the distributions of the answers given by the population groups to the first of the two questions.

Men and women did not differ in the kinds of things they selected as "the best thing the Republicans have done." It may seem surprising that women were no more likely than men to mention the end of the Korean war as the Republicans' principal achievement. This is consistent, however, with our finding in 1952 that women were no more likely to shift their vote to Eisenhower than were men, even though the Korean conflict was at that time still unsettled. Table B-6 also shows again what has been seen in many previous surveys—that women are less likely to be concerned about political issues than men. One in three of the women respondents in October 1954 would not venture an opinion as to the best thing the Republican administration had done in the previous two years.

Differences in age seemed to have very little effect on perceptions of Republican accomplishments (Table B-7). The only issue that appeared to have different implications for the different age groups was the extension of social security which understandably held a higher priority among the people over 55 than among those younger.

As we have seen in Chapter III, the major religious groups differed substantially in 1954 in the division of their vote between the two parties and these differences have also been observed in previous elections. When we look at the Protestant and Catholic respondents in Table B-8, however, we find that these two groups are very similar in their answers to the question regarding Republican achievements.

The Jewish population in the United States is so small that national surveys typically do not have enough Jewish respondents to represent this group adequately. The small Jewish sample in the present survey differed so markedly from the larger religious categories in answers to the "best thing" question, however, that it deserves comment. Aside from being more aware of political issues than the other two groups, Jews also gave quite a different order of priority to the different items mentioned. The extension of social security and the desegregation of schools received higher mention among Jews than among the other religious groups and the Korean war was much less frequently mentioned. The reduction of taxes also had high priority although it was not accompanied by an emphasis on reduction in governmental expenditures as we find to be true when educational and income levels are compared. Other research has indicated that being Jewish has much greater political implication in American society than being Protestant or being Catholic, and our present limited data sustain this finding.

In sharp contrast to the political involvement of the Jewish minority is the lack of involvement of the Negro minority (Table B-9). Almost half of this group when asked about Republican accomplishments could not think of anything. The only issue that seemed to attract particular attention from this group was the desegregation of schools and even here this response was volunteered by only one in eight of the Negro respondents. Although the Negro population is now heavily identified with the Democratic party, it is not very extensively politicized so far as issues are concerned.

The division of the sample into types of communities does not show any great differences in perceptions of the Republican party's achievements (Table B-10). People living in the metropolitan centers were somewhat less likely to single out the Korean truce for reasons that are not apparent and they seemed to be more concerned about social security than people in the other areas. In general, no meaningful patterns of response appear in this comparison.

Years of formal education is one of the most dependable variables in the armamentarium of the social scientist. It is far from a "pure" variable since it is heavily correlated with income, occupation and other measures of social status. However, it also correlates meaningfully with a wide range of the major attitudinal and behavioral variables which interest social scientists. In the present case we found (Table B-11) the contrasting educational levels differing greatly in their awareness of the activities of the Republican administration and also in their evaluation of what this administration had accomplished. College people were far more voluble on these matters than were people of less formal education and they were much more likely to speak in terms of specific issues which did not have broad national interest. They were also much concerned with reducing taxes and governmental expenditures, reflecting thereby their favored economic position. All educational groups gave the ending of the Korean war the highest priority in their list of Republican accomplishments. If we consider only those people at each educational level who were able to volunteer some specific answer to this question, however, we find that the Korean war neld much greater prominence at the lower educational levels than at the higher.

The separation of the population into occupational groups (Table B-12) results in similar comparisons to those we have seen in the educational groups. The professional, business, and white-collar groups were more likely to talk about reducing governmental expenditures and of special issues which were not referred to widely by the general population. The other groups were more likely to say they didn't know anything the Republicans had done. Special attention should be drawn to the very high proportion of farm operators who listed the ending of the Korean war as the principal Republican achievement. This tends to confirm certain indications in our 1952 study that the farm population was particularly responsive to the international crisis of that period and that the very large increase in the farm vote and its strong shift from the Democratic to the Republican party could be attributed in large part to dissatisfaction regarding the conduct of the Korean war.

The role of the labor unions in molding the attitudes of their members is a matter of considerable concern to politicians and others interested in political behavior. It is perhaps surprising to find union members' and non-members' answers to the "best thing" question differing only slightly. Considering only the laborer occupations we find in Table B-13 that union members were more likely than non-members to have a specific answer to this question rather than a mere "don't know." This may be due entirely to their predominantly Northern metropolitan residence rather than to union membership itself. There were also a good many more union members than non-members who felt that everything the Republican party had done in the previous two years was "bad." This may reflect the greater Democratic party identification of union members. Among the specific issues listed, however, there is no difference of great size except, surprisingly enough, in the proportions referring to the ending of the Korean war. Why half as many again of the union members should mention this as compared to non-members is not clear. There is no obvious reason to attribute this difference to factors associated with union membership.

The different income levels showed the same pattern of responses to the "best thing" question as was found with the different educational levels (Table B-14). The primary difference is in the ability of the high-income people to verbalize specific comments regarding Republican achievements. There is also the understandable tendency of these people to give high priority to tax reductions and reductions in governmental expenditures.

In summarizing the answers of these various population groups to our question regarding "the best thing the Republicans have done" it seems safe to conclude that no issue stood out in the public mind with great salience except the termination of the Korean war. The importance of the Korean settlement is in no way surprising since it was apparent in our 1952 study that this issue was the greatest single concern of the electorate during that campaign. As we have seen, this issue was pre-eminent among virtually all of the groups we have considered (with the exception of the Jewish sample which may have been too small for reliable comparisons). The Korean war was obviously an issue which transcended all of the usual considerations that divide people politically. It may be that foreign conflict has the unique ability to affect the American electorate as a total group whereas domestic issues are responded to differentially along income, occupational, regional and similar lines.

A second finding worthy of general comment is the fact that only three percent of the sample specifically commended the Republican party for their activities in "getting Communists out of government." No group of all those we have looked at mentioned this issue in more than five percent of the cases. This finding is consistent with the data from our 1952 study and is supported by the more recent study of Stouffer.[1] It seems apparent that public concern with Communists in government was not nearly as great as one might have surmised from the content of the information media during the 1952-54 period.

It may be pointed out that this question offers an instructive illustration of the differences to be expected from the use of open-ended questions and the more specific categorical questions customarily used by the newspaper polls. If we had asked our respondents "Do you think the administration's attempts to get Communists out of government are a good thing?" we would undoubtedly have recorded a high proportion saying "yes." In doing so we would almost certainly have overstated the public's involvement in this issue.

The Worst Thing the Republican Party Has Done

When we asked our respondents to tell us the "worst thing" the Republican party had done in its two years of tenure we received a distribution of answers which was in general complementary to those given to the previous question. The same groups that were able to comment on specific accomplishments made by the Republican party were also able to offer specific criticisms. Those who didn't know anything good to say also had nothing bad to say. Where the high-status groups had

---

1. Stouffer, Samuel A., *Communism, Conformity, and Civil Liberties*, Garden City, New York: Doubleday & Company, Inc., 1955, 5-278.

applauded the reductions in taxes and governmental expenditures, the low-status groups (unskilled labor and Negroes) criticized unemployment.   Farmers and rural people were most often badly impressed with the administration's farm program.   Union members were again quite similar to non-members although they tended to emphasize unemployment more than did non-members and also were less likely to criticize the administration's activities in the desegregation of public schools.

The item of greatest prominence in the answers to this question is the criticism of the administration's handling of Senator McCarthy.   This was the most frequently mentioned shortcoming of the Republican party and its distribution among the various population groups presents an interesting pattern.   Inspection of Tables B-15 through B-23 will show that this response, which for the most part was a criticism of the administration's failure to control the Senator's activities sufficiently, came very largely from the high-education, high-income, high-occupational status and metropolitan groups.   The differences between the high and low categories of these population dimensions are in the order of four to one.   Our small Jewish sample again shows itself to be quite different from the two larger religious groups, almost twice as many of them as of the other two groups criticizing the administration for "mishandling McCarthy."

Our inquiry did not permit us to explore fully the implications of these opinions regarding Senator McCarthy.   We do not know whether these criticisms arose from a concern over civil liberties which these people might have seen as being improperly infringed, from a distaste for a public spectacle which they had recently seen on their television screens, or from some other consideration.   Some additional information regarding this phase of the 1954 campaign will be forthcoming when we consider the specific question regarding Senator McCarthy which was asked of our respondents.

The reader will observe that in this list of criticisms very little reference was made to anything having to do with foreign affairs.   Despite the turbulent period of the 83rd Congress which saw the collapse of Northern Indo-China, the ascendance of Communist China and the various episodes and alarms involving Soviet Russia, very few of our respondents saw fit to criticize the administration's foreign policies.   One is led to suspect from this and other evidence that the American public feels uncomfortable in the face of international problems and tends to reject them from the focus of its interest.   When they were forced to live with the daily realities of international conflict during the Korean war many Americans reacted with great impatience and frustration, a state of mind which was partly responsible for the overturn of the Democratic administration in 1952.

The Performance of President Eisenhower

The influence of President Eisenhower on the 1954 congressional election would be extremely difficult to assess. His name did not appear on the ballot and he was not even a very active campaigner. However, his personality appears to have been such an important factor in the 1952 campaign and was so closely associated with the political fortunes of the Republican party at the time of this study that it was felt desirable to make some attempt to add to our information regarding the public image of the President. Two questions regarding Mr. Eisenhower were asked, both referring to his two years as president. The first of these read:

"Has Mr. Eisenhower turned out to be as good a president as you thought he would or have you been disappointed in him?"

About two-thirds of the sample responded to this question by saying that President Eisenhower had turned out as well as they had expected, a few of these going further and saying that he had turned out even better than expected. We do not know what value to attach to these absolute figures since we have no previous data to which they can be compared. A more interesting approach is to look at the one person in five who expressed himself as disappointed in the President and to find out where these people were located in the various levels of the electorate.

We find in the first place (Table B-24) that men and women did not differ significantly in their answers to this question. This is an added demonstration of the fact that men and women did not react very differently to Mr. Eisenhower as a political figure despite the contention of some who have held that Mr. Eisenhower was especially attractive to the women voters. We also see that the different age groups did not answer this question differently, a finding similar to that obtained with the two previous questions (Table B-25).

Catholics and Jews both reported greater disappointment with Mr. Eisenhower than did Protestants (Table B-26). This no doubt reflects the greater Democratic bias of these two

68

religious groups, criticism of the President being clearly associated with party identification as we will see in Chapter VI. Negro and white respondents differed only slightly in their answers to this question (Table B-27).

The most interesting item which emerges when we compare types of communities is the very high rating given Mr. Eisenhower by rural people (Table B-28). It is not surprising that the President stood well in the suburban areas where the Republican vote was high in 1954 but his popularity in the rural areas is less easily understood.

When we look at the responses of the educational divisions we find the interesting fact that disappointment with Mr. Eisenhower's first two years of office increased with educational level (Table B-29). Despite the fact that people of grade-school training split their votes about equally between Eisenhower and Stevenson in 1952 while people of college training voted over two to one for Eisenhower, criticism of Mr. Eisenhower expressed in our October 1954 survey was most frequent among the latter group. Consistent with this is the fact that among the occupational groups it was the high-status professional and businessman category that expressed the most frequent disappointment with the President (Table B-30). The high incidence of criticism among these groups may simply reflect a keener awareness among these relatively well-informed people of whatever shortcomings the Eisenhower administration may have had. The other occupational groups did not differ greatly with the exception of farmers who appeared to be most generally satisfied.

Union membership does not appear to have been a very significant consideration in determining responses to this question (Table B-31). The proportion of union members who did not expect much from Mr. Eisenhower in the first place was larger than that of non-members, with the consequence that union members were somewhat less likely to express satisfaction with him. The differences were not great, however, with a large majority of both groups expressing no disappointment. The income groups (Table B-32), interestingly enough, did not reflect the progression which we have seen in the educational groups. The distributions of satisfaction and disappointment were virtually identical for all three of the income brackets considered.

Our second question pertaining to Mr. Eisenhower's performance as president read as follows:

"Would you say that Mr. Eisenhower has been a better than average president, just about average, or not as good as average?"

This question gives us a somewhat wider division of answers than did the previous one with the result that while two-thirds of the sample seemed to be satisfied with Mr. Eisenhower's performance in office almost as large a number spoke of him as "just about average" as president. Without entangling ourselves in a discussion of what the precise meaning of the term "average" is we can look at the characteristics of those people who regarded Mr. Eisenhower as either better or poorer than average.

Men and women again did not differ greatly although women were a little less willing to be harsh in their estimation of the President (Table B-33). The different age groups were also similar although for reasons not immediately apparent the over 55 category was somewhat more inclined to give him a better-than-average rating (Table B-34).

Catholic and Jewish respondents expressed themselves in the same terms as they had in the previous question (Table B-35), being somewhat more critical than Protestants. The Jewish group had the closest balance of better-than-average to poorer-than-average ratings with a somewhat larger number of mixed and qualified answers than were given by the other two groups. In contrast to the previous question Negro respondents were clearly more inclined to grade the President down than were white respondents (Table B-36).

Suburban people were clearly the most willing to rate the President as "better than average" (Table B-37). Criticism was most common in the metropolitan centers. Rural people were strongly inclined to use the conservative estimate of "average" in answering this question but, consistent with their answers to the previous question, they very seldom rated the President as "poorer than average. "

Although college people, as we have seen, were more likely to express themselves as disappointed with Mr. Eisenhower than the other educational levels, they were more inclined to grade him high in comparison to the average president (Table B-38). Although people of only grade-school training were about as likely to call Mr. Eisenhower a poorer-than-average president as a better-than-average one, the ratio favoring the latter answer increases as formal education increases and among college people the relation of favorable estimates to unfavorable ones was in the order of five to one. A similar high rating is seen in the professional, business and other white-collar occu-pational groups (Table B-39). Skilled and unskilled laborers, on the other hand, gave the President about an equal balance of above average and below average ratings. Farmers answered this question in about the same way they had answered the previous one, with a large majority assigning him a rating of average and a very small number calling him poorer-than-average.

Union members were less likely to rate the President favorably than people who did not belong to unions (Table B-40). When we consider only the members of the skilled and unskilled labor categories, however, we find that union membership did not differentiate our respondents in their answers to this question. Both union and non-union members of these occupations gave the President a relatively low rating compared to the other population groups. The division by income status shows the same high evaluation of the President in the over $6000 category that we have seen in the high educational and occupational groups (Table B-41).

In attempting to interpret the limited data which we have obtained from these two questions we may first observe that the amount of direct criticism of President Eisenhower does not appear to have been very great. While a visible minority (19 percent) felt that he had not come up to their pre-election expectation this did not mean necessarily that they did not still think well of him. Although we have no previous data to use as a base line, the rating of ten percent who described the President as poorer-than-average is obviously close to the ultimate minimum that any president can hope to achieve.

There is ample reason to believe from these data and from other evidence that at the time this survey was taken the American public was favorably disposed toward President Eisenhower. In the common parlance he was "popular." What are the political implications of this popularity? It is apparent that the President's personal appeal was not sufficient to swing the 1954 congressional election to the Republican party. It may be argued that had Mr. Eisenhower not been the head of the Republican party the Republican candidates for Congress would have fared much worse than they actually did. We have seen that there were more defections in 1954 among Democratic identifiers than among Republican and we have suggested that this may have resulted from Mr. Eisenhower's influence. This is a plausible hypothesis although not proved.

As we attempted to show in our 1952 study, candidate appeal is only one of the forces that move the voters and in an off-year congressional election this aspect of political motivation is probably relatively weak since many of the national leaders are not on the ballot. Issues of a partisan character may enter strongly into such a situation and swing the vote one way or the other. If they do not, and they apparently did not in 1954, then considerations of party loyalty assume transcendent importance and the decision rests largely on which party can muster a larger number of its followers to the polls.

Expected Effect of the Election on Personal Finances

We turn now to the four specific questions regarding political issues. The first asked the respondents whether they thought it would make any difference to them financially if the Democrats or the Republicans won the election. Over half of the respondents said they did not feel the election would affect their families financially, but of those who did approximately two out of three thought they would be better off if the Democrats won (Table B-42). When we compare this to our 1952 findings with the same question we see that more people saw financial implications in the outcome of the presidential election than was the case in the following congressional election, and that again those who saw a difference were more likely to say they would be better off if the Democrats won.

Our two previous election surveys have documented the widely-held stereotype of the Democratic party as the party of the common man and the Republican party as the party of the privileged. Although our present question did not pose the issue in these terms an inspection of the answers given by the various population groups makes clear who saw a victory of one or the other party as financially beneficial and who did not. As we see from Table B-43 through B-51 the greatest expectations of financial benefit from a Democratic victory are found in the less-privileged classes, Negroes, unskilled workers, and people of low income. Skilled laborers and farmers also showed a heavy preference for the Democratic party in their answers to this question. The high-status groups, college-educated, high-income, professional and white-collar occupations were somewhat less likely to feel that the election would have any effect on them financially, and those who did see the election as making a difference were about as likely to see benefits in the victory of one party as the other. It is noteworthy that none of the groups in our tables were more likely to see themselves getting

72

along better financially in the event of a Republican rather than a Democratic victory.

In reviewing these data the reader may wonder how it comes about that a group, such as farmers, voted in 1954 about equally for Democratic and Republican candidates although they were considerably more likely to see a Democratic victory as financially advantageous to them than a Republican one. There appear to be two answers to this apparent contradiction. In the first place it is likely from what we have seen in Chapter IV that those farmers who felt they would be better off if the Democrats won were considerably less likely to vote than the average of their group. Secondly, it is very likely that some people voted Republican although they answered this question with a Democratic preference. It may be assumed that during a period of prosperity economic considerations may not be so pressing and political decisions may be influenced more heavily by other factors than they would be during a time of economic stress. We would expect, in other words, that during a period of severe depression the answers to this question would more closely parallel the actual vote than they did in the 1954 survey.

U.S. Involvement in World Affairs

The limitations of our survey restricted us to a single question in the area of public attitudes toward international affairs:

> "Some people think that since the end of the last world war this country has gone too far in concerning itself with problems in other parts of the world. How do you feel about this?"

It is obvious that public thinking on the complicated issues of international affairs cannot be adequately represented by the answers to this or any other one question. An intensive investigation of public opinion regarding foreign affairs is badly needed. The question quoted above has been used by the Survey Research Center in a number of earlier studies and is known to correlate with a number of other questions intended to bring out the relative willingness of people to see this country involved with or isolated from foreign countries.

We know from earlier research that the most dependable correlate of internationalist attitudes is education and we see this expressed sharply in Table B-57. A heavy majority of college people rejected the statement that this country has "gone too far" in concerning itself with world problems while people of lesser formal education were more likely to accept the statement than not. As might be expected the "not too involved" response was also given by majorities of the high-income (Table B-60) and high-occupational-status groups (Table B-58). Our small Jewish sample again showed its individuality by a high majority supporting this position (Table B-54).

Isolationist attitudes, insofar as this question measures them, are found most strongly among older people (Table B-53), Negroes (Table B-55), rural people (Table B-56), unskilled laborers, and people of low education and income. Women appear to be slightly less international in their viewpoint than men (Table B-52). It is of interest to see in Table B-59 that whatever effects union membership may have on attitudes regarding domestic issues, its influence on the kind of attitude represented in this question seems to be nil.

If any generalization may be drawn from these data it is that internationalist attitudes reflect a rather sophisticated point of view. People whose personal acquaintance with foreign countries or people from abroad is limited, whose daily lives are circumscribed and parochial, and who do not easily broaden their experience by reading or other intellectual pursuits are likely to have a narrow world view and to be apprehensive regarding American involvement with other nations. Although sophistication regarding the world outside the United States by no means guarantees a favorable attitude toward internationalist foreign policies, it seems to make it easier for a person to understand and accept the prospect of his country concerning itself with world problems.

It is clear from Table B-61, however, that the answers to our question are not simply a matter of education and breadth of experience. We see in that table wide fluctuations in the distributions of answers given by national samples interviewed by the Survey Research Center in 1948, 1952 and 1954. The sharp increase in the proportion of "this country has gone too far", responses from 1948 to 1952 undoubtedly reflects public anxiety over the Korean war. The 1954 distribution moves back toward the pre-Korean figures but does not attain the high level of that relatively peaceful period. In other words attitudes on international affairs are responsive to international events.[1]

---

1. A similar phenomenon is described in Stouffer's report on attitudes toward political nonconformists. He finds that tolerance toward various forms of nonconformity is highly correlated with educational level but that the events of the McCarthy period had moved people of all educational levels toward the intolerant end of his scale.

The Democratic period of the 1930s and 40s saw the development of a broad program of federal legislation leading to a variety of governmental activities in the field of social welfare. Opinions of the proper extent of this type of legislation have been rather heated and have tended to divide along party lines with Democrats being generally more expansive than Republicans.

The answers given by the different segments of the population to the one question in our survey dealing with social legislation were relatively predictable. As we see in Tables B-62 through B-70 those groups who might see themselves benefiting directly from the kinds of legislation proposed in the question were most likely to feel that more such legislation would be a good thing. Thus, relatively few Negroes, skilled or unskilled laborers, low-education or low-income people felt that the government had gone too far in this kind of activity and sizable proportions of these groups felt that more would be desirable. On the other hand groups who might reasonably feel that they were being asked to help pay the costs of social programs from which they did not receive any direct return were much more likely to feel that the government had already gone too far with this kind of legislation. Here we find the high-status educational, occupational and income groups.

Farmers present a case of special interest. While a relatively large proportion of this group felt that the extent of the governmental programs had been "about right" there were as many who felt the government had gone too far as felt it should go further. We do not know to what extent farmers thought of the price-support program as included in the intention of the question; probably not many. In any case farmers were the least likely of any of the occupational groups to approve the extension of social welfare programs by the federal government.

Our small Jewish sample also stands out in giving one of the highest votes of approval for continuing and extended social legislation. Since the Jewish respondents were not economically underprivileged as a group, this extreme position appears to derive from the general political philosophy which we have seen in various tables to characterize this small segment of the population.

We would certainly not be justified in coming to any fixed conclusions regarding the economic philosophy of the public on the basis of answers to this single question. However, the data we have seen, along with confirmatory evidence from other surveys,[1] are sufficient to justify the generalization that the people at large are not as apprehensive regarding the extended activities of the Federal Government as are many party leaders and political theorists. None of the population groups we have examined had more than a 20 percent minority who seemed to be willing to retrench from present levels of social legislation. The propriety of the Federal Government taking a direct hand in the solution of broad social problems appears to be widely accepted in public thinking. No doubt our sample would have reacted much less favorably if the activities proposed in the question had been labeled as "socialistic." The fact seems to be that most people do not identify governmental programs regarding unemployment, education, and housing as evidences of socialism.

When we compare these 1954 results to the answers to the same question in our 1952 survey, a shift is seen which seems to derive directly from the change in government which intervened between the two studies (Table B-71). If we assume that the Republican administration was seen by the public during its first two years of office as less expansive in sponsoring social legislation than were its Democratic predecessors, then it is reasonable to expect an increase in the proportion of our sample who feel that more should be done. If the distribution had not shifted with the change in governmental policy we would have to conclude that the public had also moved in a conservative direction along with the new administration, and this apparently did not happen.

Attitudes toward Senator McCarthy

During the period prior to the 1954 election Senator Joseph McCarthy of Wisconsin was perhaps the most controversial figure on the American political scene. We sought to obtain some indication of public reaction to the Senator through the following question:

"If you knew that Senator McCarthy was supporting a candidate for Congress would you be more likely to

---

1. See *Big Business as the People See It* Fisher, B.R., and Withey, S. B., Ann Arbor, Michigan: Survey Research Center, University of Michigan 1951, 207 pp.

vote for that candidate or less likely or wouldn't it make any difference to you?"

We see from Tables B-72 through B-80 that the various population groups present a pattern of responses to this question which is quite unlike those given to any of the previous ones. In the first place, it is apparent that Senator McCarthy had a special appeal to the Catholic section of the population (Table B-74). Even among this group the proportion who responded positively to the Senator was no larger than that which responded negatively. But it is the highest positive response he received in any of the groups we have examined. Our Jewish sample on the other hand was far and away the most antagonistic in its answers to our question. Despite the prominence of certain Jewish associates of the Senator, our Jewish respondents rejected him by a ratio of nine to one over those who gave him their approval.

We might have expected that since Senator McCarthy is a Republican the high status groups, where Republicans are most frequent, would have been most likely to approve the Senator's activities. The opposite is clearly the case. As educational, occupational and income levels rise, disapproval of Senator McCarthy also rises (Tables B-77, B-78 and B-80). It may be noted that these high status groups tended also to have a slightly higher proportion of people who approved of Senator McCarthy. These groups appear to have reacted more strongly to the Senator, both positively and negatively, than did the less well-informed sections of the population.

The McCarthy issue is one of the few we have seen in which union members responded differently than did non-members of similar occupations (Table B-79). Whether because of labor union indoctrination or other factors, union members were more likely to disapprove of the Senator than were those not associated with unions. Rural people, including farmers, appeared to have been relatively less involved in the political problems associated with Senator McCarthy. As with the other groups, however, those who had some reaction to the Senator were more likely to be disapproving than approving (B-76).

What conclusion can we draw from the fact that all of these population groupings with the single exception of Catholics were much more likely to be unfavorable in their reaction to Senator McCarthy's activities than to be favorable? It is unfortunate that the limitations of our survey did not permit us to probe into the motivations which lay behind these evaluations. Our data are sufficient, however, to make it apparent that the political influence which Senator McCarthy exerted on the American electorate just prior to the 1954 election was grossly misjudged in many quarters. In spite of the tremendous publicity given Senator McCarthy by the information media during this period, in spite of the Committee of a Million and the various other expressions of public support, and in spite of the deference shown him in high places, when we interviewed our national sample in October 1954 we found that in so far as the public held opinions regarding Senator McCarthy they were overwhelmingly disapproving.

It has sometimes been said that public opinion surveys may serve the function in a democratic society of demonstrating which of the many pressures that are brought to bear on public officials spring from genuine public support and which are supported by only a "phantom public." We appear to have an instance of their ability to discriminate fact and phantom in the case of the public and Senator McCarthy.

Summary

The purpose of Chapter V has been to find the extent to which political attitudes appear to derive from position in the population. We have been interested in establishing whether there is a woman's point of view, a Catholic point of view, a farmer's point of view, or any other point of view on political matters which is associated with population group membership.

The answer to our question must be a qualified one. We have seen that there are some segments of the population that differed consistently from the other groups in their expressed attitudes on the issues we presented. Outstanding among these is the group of college-educated people. This highly select minority (18 percent) were more likely than other people to have an opinion on the issues we raised and their opinions differed from those of the others. They rated the Republican party and President Eisenhower more highly, they were more conservative on economic policies, more internationalist on foreign policy, and more critical of Senator McCarthy. In part this orientation may reflect the same social class theme which we saw in our analysis of voting but it is clear that it has broader implications than those of a purely economic nature.

The other group who seem to have a highly developed political individuality are people of the Jewish religion. We have

78

pointed out the discrepant character of many of their attitudes in the text of this chapter. Their orientation has some components common to the college pattern but it differs markedly in its emphasis on "liberal" social and economic legislation.

Aside from these two rather unusual groups we do not find consistent patterns in the attitudes we have measured. The high-status occupational and income groups tend to show an orientation similar to the college group but it is not as distinct, possibly because these groups are more heterogeneous in composition. There are several instances of partial patterns, distinct positions on some issues but not on others. Union members are an example. Their views on the government's economic activities are consistent and more "liberal" than those of unorganized labor. They also follow the union leadership in their disapproval of Senator McCarthy. But there is no union position regarding foreign affairs which differs from that of non-union labor, at least so far as our survey could measure it.

Finally there are a number of examples of groups which seem to have no organized orientation on the political issues we presented but do have an idiosyncratic response to some particular issue which has specific relevance to them. Catholics are a case in point. They differed very little from Protestants in the tables we have presented except in the case of Senator McCarthy. This issue, which obviously had special significance for Catholics, divided them sharply from Protestants. A further example is older people. They differed very little from the younger age groups except in one item, their greater interest in social security.

Although our data on issues are limited they suggest the following conclusions:

1. Most of the major population groups which make up the American electorate are not characterized by highly patterned orientations regarding political issues although many individual members of these groups doubtless have strong political views.

2. Those population groups which most closely approximate patterned orientations on political issues are groups which in some important respect are relatively homogeneous within their own membership, relatively distinct from the rest of the population, and relatively sophisticated regarding political affairs. Even in these groups many individuals do not conform to the group pattern.

79

3. The broader and more heterogeneous the group, the less likely it is to hold political views in common. Thus dividing the population on the basis of sex or age does not reveal significant differences in viewpoints on general issues.

4. Some groups which do not show a pattern of attitudes do respond to a specific issue which they recognize as having particular relevance for them. Such issues have clear implications of self-interest for the individual group members.

If we look back at the tables in Chapter III and compare them to those in the present chapter we find that the various population groups differ more in their voting than they do in their attitudes on political issues. There is a rough correspondence between individuality in vote and in attitudes, with the groups which were most partisan in their vote tending to be the most one-sided in their attitudes. This suggests that for these groups votes and attitudes are related components of some general political orientation. This has also been indicated by the findings of previous studies by the Survey Research Center and others that Republican and Democratic voters differ in their responses to various issue questions.

The general factor which underlies these consistent, albeit imperfect, relationships between votes and attitudes may take different forms. For some people it may be basic values regarding freedom, equality, fair play or the like. For others there may be well organized social or political ideologies. For some, political attitudes and decisions may be determined by some underlying trait of personality. It may also be that for some people, and especially in some issue areas, attitudes relate to votes because both derive from a personal identification with one or the other of the two major parties.

In Chapter VI we will examine the responses given by the different party identification groups in answer to our issue questions. This will tell us which of the issues we have considered actually had partisan significance in the 1954 campaign and whether the relationship between party identification and attitudes on these issues conforms to our expectations.

VI

THE ATTITUDES OF THE PARTY IDENTIFICATION GROUPS

We have seen in Chapter III that party identification was highly related to probable vote in the 1954 election. The direction of party attachment (Republican or Democratic) was associated with the choice of candidates running for Congress; the degree of identification was also an important factor. Strong party identifiers were considerably more likely to prefer the candidate of their party than were weak identifiers.

The concept of party identification, as we have defined it, implies a personal sense of belonging to one or the other of the major political parties. We have proposed that this psychological attachment is one of the major forces which determines the behavior of voters on Election Day. We have also suggested that this factor will have effects not only in voting preferences but also in the stands the individual citizen takes on political issues. It is our belief that the party serves a standard-setting function for its followers, that conformity to this standard will be most apparent on issues which are most clearly party-related, and that strong party identifiers will conform more closely to their "party line" than will weak identifiers.

The questions regarding the issues and personalities prominent during the 1954 campaign provide us data which are relevant to these hypotheses. Our inquiry was not sufficiently broad to give us a full picture of the degree to which a party position on issues exists among the Republican and Democratic rank-and-file. However, it can provide partial answers to the questions we are asking: Do followers of the two parties take visibly different positions on issues; On what kinds of issues are these differences greatest; and, Are the differences largest among people whose party identification is strongest?

81

In examining the data presented in this chapter the reader will remember from Chapter II that identification with the two parties varies substantially in the different income, educational, religious, and other groups. This suggests that differences among Democratic and Republican identifiers on the question regarding welfare legislation, for example, might be a reflection of income differences rather than party differences. In order to eliminate this ambiguity all of the tables presented in this chapter have been broken down to show differences between identifiers of the two parties within homogeneous demographic categories (low income, college education, Catholic, etc.). Although these data are too voluminous to present in this report, they will be referred to in connection with each of the interview questions considered.

The Performance of the Republican Party

As we have seen, each of the 1139 respondents in the sample was asked two questions pertaining to the activities of the Republican administration. Table VI-1 presents the distribution of responses to the question as to "the best thing the Republican party has done" when the total sample is divided according to party identification. Three items in this table are of interest:

● The ending of the Korean war appears to have had a bipartisan appeal among our sample. Respondents of both party persuasions and of different degrees of party identification gave this achievement about equal emphasis. This finding almost two years after the conclusion of the Korean war demonstrates again the transcendent impact of that conflict and supports the conclusion drawn from our earlier research that this issue played a dominant role in the 1952 campaign and contributed heavily to the defeat of the Democratic party in that election.

● Although none of the other accomplishments credited to the Republican administration was supported by more than a small proportion of the sample, one appears to have a clearly partisan flavor, the reduction of governmental expenditures. While only three percent of the self-styled Democrats cited this as the best performance of the Republican administration, it was selected by eight percent of the weak Republicans and 13 percent of the strong Republicans. In other words, cutting of governmental expenditures has the character of a partisan issue. As we will see in Table VI-7 this conclusion is supported by the data coming from our question on governmental welfare activities.

82

● Although only six percent of our respondents went so far as to reject the intent of our question by stating that nothing the Republicans had done in their two years in office could be called good, this response came almost entirely from Democrats and much more frequently from strong party identifiers than from weak ones. Our thinking regarding the influence of party identification would be seriously compromised if these data had come out otherwise.

Table VI-1

RELATION OF PARTY IDENTIFICATION TO
"THE BEST THING THE REPUBLICANS HAVE DONE"

"What would you say is the best thing the Republican party has done since it took over the government two years ago?"

	Strong Democrat	Weak Democrat	Inde-pendent Democrat	Inde-pendent	Inde-pendent Repub-lican	Weak Repub-lican	Strong Repub-lican
Ended Korean War	25%	28%	21%	21%	40%	34%	32%
Reduced taxes	6	8	6	7	6	11	8
Reduced govern-mental expenditures	3	3	7	5	12	8	13
Extended social security	6	5	9	7	1	5	6
Got Communists out of government	2	1	4	4	3	5	4
Desegregated schools	3	5	1	--	--	4	1
Other	12	12	21	17	24	18	16
Don't know	28	32	22	35	13	15	19
Everything bad	15	6	9	4	1	--	1
	100%	100%	100%	100%	100%	100%	100%
Number of cases	248	288	97	82	68	159	146

Looking now at the second question regarding the perform-ance of the Republican party we again find interesting party dif-ferences. The reader will recall that this question read:

"What would you say is the worst thing the Republican party has done in the last two years?"

The most intriguing finding in Table VI-2 is the fact that Republicans were twice as likely to criticize their own party for mishandling Senator McCarthy as were Democrats and in most cases this criticism implied disapproval of the Senator himself.

This is particularly interesting in view of the fact that in answer to our direct question (see Table VI-8) Republicans, especially strong Republicans, showed themselves more favorably disposed to the Senator than were Democrats, especially strong Democrats. Our data are not sufficiently detailed to give us a convincing explanation of this apparent paradox. We find, however, that the selection of the McCarthy problem as the "worst thing" the Republican administration had done was about three times as frequent among the high-income and high-education Republicans as it was among Republicans of lower income and educational rank, whereas the distributions of approval and disapproval of McCarthy—as expressed to the direct question—did not differ among Republicans of these different levels. This may mean that Republicans of greater political sensitivity felt that the publicity regarding Senator McCarthy, particularly in connection with his feud with the Army, was hurting the Republican party. Their criticism may have been directed as much toward the leadership of the party for letting this happen as it was toward Senator McCarthy himself. Aside from this party consideration they seemed no differently disposed toward the Senator than Republicans of other status levels.

The relative silence of Democrats in the face of the McCarthy attacks on their party is perplexing. Although they reacted unfavorably to him as an individual much more commonly than Republicans did (Table VI-8) they were less likely to criticize the Republican party for his activities than were Republicans themselves. Were Democrats intimidated by Senator McCarthy's aggressive behavior, were they repressing a subject which they found embarrassing, or were they simply less responsive to the Senator's activities? We do not have a satisfactory answer.

The one specific issue which shows clearly partisan characteristics in the responses to the "worst thing" question is unemployment. There was not a high level of unemployment in 1954 and only four percent of our sample offered this as their major criticism. But this was almost exclusively a Democratic response and was particularly concentrated among strong Democrats. This finding is perhaps most significant in suggesting the readiness of Democrats to react to the issue of unemployment if it were to become more salient.

One of eight of our respondents wouldn't accept the suggestion that the Republican administration had done anything that could be called "worst." This was the most party-connected answer of all those recorded. Republicans outdid Democrats by a considerable margin in saying everything the Republicans

had done had been good and when we consider only strong identifiers the difference is in the order of five to one. Of course
this finding was to be expected and it illustrates again the quality
of party loyalty.

The comparison of party groups differing in the major demographic characteristics does not change any of these conclusions.
Differences exist between demographic groups, as we saw in
Chapter V, but with the exceptions noted above party differences
are comparable from one demographic level to another.

Table VI-2

RELATION OF PARTY IDENTIFICATION TO
"THE WORST THING THE REPUBLICANS HAVE DONE"

	"What would you say is the worst thing the Republican party has done in the last two years?"						
	Strong Democrat	Weak Democrat	Inde-pendent Democrat	Inde-pendent	Inde-pendent Repub-lican	Weak Repub-lican	Strong Repub-lican
Mishandled McCarthy	7%	11%	14%	11%	22%	18%	20%
Poor farm program	4	8	7	4	4	6	3
Unemployment	10	3	3	4	4	2	--
Poor tax program	6	2	7	6	4	3	3
Desegregated schools	6	3	4	6	--	3	3
Too lenient toward Russia	2	2	5	--	6	2	2
Other	30	18	19	16	18	16	16
Don't know	30	42	25	46	32	37	29
Everything good	5	11	16	7	10	13	24
	100%	100%	100%	100%	100%	100%	100%
Number of cases	248	288	97	82	68	159	146

The Performance of President Eisenhower

Our 1952 study provided ample documentation of the personal
influence which Mr. Eisenhower exerted on the voters in that
election, including many whose usual party attachment was Democratic. Our two questions regarding the President's performance in office give us an opportunity to see to what extent adherents of the two parties saw the President differently at the
time of the 1954 election.

The answers to both questions were highly correlated with
party identification. When asked if they were satisfied or disap-

pointed in Mr. Eisenhower as president only one Republican in seven expressed any criticism of the President while more than one out of three Democrats did (Table VI-3). Strong Democrats were especially critical, almost half either saying they were disappointed or hadn't expected much in the first place. Strong Republicans may have been a little more favorable than weak Republicans, although both groups were very high in their approval.

The ratings of Mr. Eisenhower as a "better-than-average, about average, or not as good as average" president show the same marked party differences and even sharper differences between the weak and strong adherents of the two parties (Table VI-4). It is clear that strong Democrats saw the President in a very different light than did strong Republicans.

Levels of approval and disapproval differ somewhat among the major population groups (as we saw in Chapter V) but within these groups Republicans and Democrats are very consistent in answering these two questions. Republicans are more favorable than Democrats, strong identifiers more extreme in their positions than weak.

It was our expectation that these data regarding Mr. Eisenhower would show the pattern we have seen. In our 1951 study of party identification we stated, "Assuming that reference to persons prominent in the parties gives the sharpest definition of party position, it is perhaps not surprising to find that questions which personalize the party conflict produce the greatest difference in the responses of the party adherents." Mr. Eisenhower was clearly the leader of the Republican party in 1954, and he was clearly a highly partisan figure in the public mind.

Effect of the Election on Personal Finances

We found in Table B-42 that a larger proportion of the public felt they would be better off financially with a Democratic administration than with a Republican one. We now see in Table VI-5 that this is a highly partisan issue. Very few followers of either party were willing to say that they would be better off if the other party should win. Democrats especially were committed to the belief that their financial well-being would be best entrusted to their party.

Here again we find the strong party identifiers, both Republican and Democratic, to be markedly more partisan in their views than the weak party followers. High party loyalty seems to increase the need for defense of one's own group.

86

Table VI-3

RELATION OF PARTY IDENTIFICATION TO SATISFACTION WITH EISENHOWER

	"Has Mr. Eisenhower turned out to be as good a president as you thought he would or have you been disappointed in him?"						
	Strong Democrat	Weak Democrat	Independent Democrat	Independent	Independent Republican	Weak Republican	Strong Republican
As good as or better than expected	47%	65%	55%	73%	78%	79%	85%
As expected, but didn't expect much	17	7	10	6	1	3	1
Expectations not fulfilled, but not disappointed	--	4	2	1	1	3	1
Disappointed	30	17	28	13	15	12	10
Other responses	6	7	5	7	5	3	3
	100%	100%	100%	100%	100%	100%	100%
Number of cases	248	288	97	82	68	159	146

Table VI-4

RELATION OF PARTY IDENTIFICATION TO RATING OF EISENHOWER

	"Would you say Mr. Eisenhower has been a better-than-average president, just about average, or not as good as average?"						
	Strong Democrat	Weak Democrat	Independent Democrat	Independent	Independent Republican	Weak Republican	Strong Republican
Better than average	6%	17%	21%	20%	34%	33%	54%
Average	61	72	62	66	56	58	42
Poorer than average	24	7	13	6	6	4	2
Other responses	9	4	4	8	4	5	2
	100%	100%	100%	100%	100%	100%	100%
Number of cases	248	288	97	82	68	159	146

When we look at Republicans and Democrats within different income and educational levels we find that the general pattern holds quite consistently although there was some tendency for the lower status Democrats to emphasize the financial advantages of a Democratic victory and for the higher-status Republicans to stress the advantage of a Republican victory. It is of interest that none of the rural groups gave the Republican party a strong vote of confidence on this question. Even strong Republicans among rural people were much less likely than their urban and metropolitan co-partisans to see a Republican victory as meaning financial advantage to them.

Table VI-5

RELATION OF PARTY IDENTIFICATION TO EXPECTED FINANCIAL EFFECT
OF THE ELECTION

	"Do you think it will make any difference in how you and your family get along financially whether the Democrats or Republicans win?"						
	Strong Democrat	Weak Democrat	Independent Democrat	Independent	Independent Republican	Weak Republican	Strong Republican
Better off if Democrats win	52%	23%	21%	12%	7%	5%	3%
Won't make any difference	38	65	74	68	57	74	55
Better off if Republicans win	4	5	1	9	29	11	36
Don't know	6	7	4	11	7	10	6
	100%	100%	100%	100%	100%	100%	100%
Number of cases	248	288	97	82	68	159	146

U.S. Involvement in World Affairs

As we see in Table VI-6, groups of different party identification did not differ substantially in their answers to our question as to whether "this country has gone too far in concerning itself with problems in other parts of the world." The distribution does not conform to our expectation for a partisan issue.

In view of the fact that our 1951 and 1952 studies have shown a clear relationship between attitudes on foreign policy issues and party choice this finding is somewhat surprising. The explanation becomes apparent when we compare Table VI-6 to an identical table taken from our 1952 study (Figure VI-1). We now find that the shift in responses to this question which occurred between 1952 and 1954 was almost entirely accounted for by the Republican identifiers. While they had held by a two-to-one majority in 1952 that this country had "gone too far" in its foreign involvements, in 1954 they rejected this statement by a small majority. Strong Republicans moved further from their original position than did weak Republicans. Democratic identifiers, in contrast, changed scarcely at all in the two surveys.

Table VI-6

RELATION OF PARTY IDENTIFICATION TO U. S. INVOLVEMENT
IN WORLD AFFAIRS

"Some people think that since the end of the last world war this
country has gone too far in concerning itself with problems in
other parts of the world.   How do you feel about this?"

	Strong Democrat	Weak Democrat	Inde- pendent Democrat	Inde- pendent	Inde- pendent Repub- lican	Weak Repub- lican	Strong Repub- lican
Too much involved	49%	45%	28%	43%	41%	41%	43%
Pro-con, depends	3	3	3	4	--	4	1
Not too much involved	40	44	65	40	57	48	49
Other responses	8	8	4	13	2	7	7
	100%	100%	100%	100%	100%	100%	100%
Number of cases	248	288	97	82	68	159	146

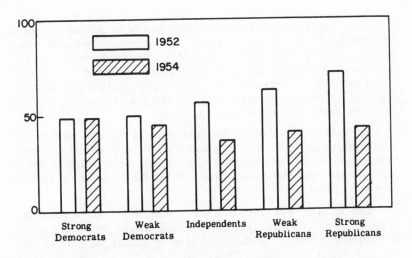

Figure VI-1. Proportions of Party Groups Stating this
Country Has Gone too Far in Concerning
Itself with World Problems: 1952—1954.

While we cannot make any general statements regarding attitudes on foreign policy on the basis of a single question, the data we have presented suggest support of the hypothesis proposed in our 1951 study that "for many people Democratic or Republican attitudes regarding foreign policy result from conscious or unconscious adherence to a perceived party line, rather than from influences independent of party identification." It would seem clear that the ascension of Mr. Eisenhower to the leadership of the Republican party in 1952 swung the party-line strongly in the direction of an "internationalist" view of foreign affairs. Although our data are very limited, they indicate that he carried a sizable number of the party following with him.

It has repeatedly been found in surveys of public opinion that internationalist attitudes are more common among the higher-income and higher-education groups. As we saw in Chapter V, this was also true in the present study and we now see that it was true of both Republicans and Democrats. The influence of education is especially marked, with grade school Democrats and Republicans both tending to accept the isolationist implication of our question and college people of both parties rejecting it strongly.

Social Legislation

As we have observed earlier, the question of governmental action in the field of social welfare has been one of the most prominent of the partisan issues during recent national campaigns. Whether phrased in terms of "government interference," "creeping socialism," or some other more moderate terms, the issue has been a persistent one with clear party positions. It would be surprising indeed if Republicans and Democrats did not differ in their answers to our question.

As Table VI-7 shows, the followers of the two parties did differ substantially in their responses and in the expected directions. Moreover, strong party identifiers were more extreme than weak identifiers in each case. Thus the issue has a clearly partisan character.

The reader will recall from Table B-71 that a somewhat smaller proportion of the 1954 sample stated that the Federal Government should do less in the area of social legislation than we had found in 1952. This shift turns out to have occurred mainly among Republicans (data not shown) who were apparently less willing to criticize the "national government" when it was a Republican government than when it was Democratic.

90

Table VI-7

"Some people think the national government should do more in trying to deal with such problems as unemployment, education, housing and so on. Others think that the government is already doing too much. On the whole would you say that what the government is doing is about right, too much, or not enough?"

	Strong Democrat	Weak Democrat	Inde- pendent Democrat	Inde- pendent	Inde- pendent Repub- lican	Weak Repub- lican	Strong Repub- lican
Definitely should do more	10%	3%	1%	9%	6%	3%	3%
Should do more	31	17	22	26	32	19	8
Doing about right	38	55	55	34	35	45	50
Should do less	3	6	3	6	9	11	14
Definitely should do less	1	2	1	1	3	4	8
More on some, less on others	11	10	7	13	7	9	9
Other responses	6	7	11	11	8	9	8
	100%	100%	100%	100%	100%	100%	100%
Number of cases	248	288	97	82	68	159	146

The party differences within income and educational groups are highly consistent. Low-income Republicans reacted to the question very differently than low-income Democrats but very much the same as high-income Republicans. High-income Democrats were somewhat more conservative than low-income Democrats but less so than high-income Republicans. Educational differences conformed to the basic partisan pattern, with the sharpest differences being seen among people with some college education.

Attitudes toward Senator McCarthy

As we have observed earlier, Senator McCarthy was the subject of a great deal of public attention at the time of our survey. His highly publicized activities attracted more public criticism than any other event associated with the Republican party, especially among Republican identifiers.

Our direct question regarding Senator McCarthy was phrased in terms of his estimated influence on the respondent's vote for congressman:

"If you knew that Senator McCarthy was supporting a candidate for Congress would you be more likely to vote for that candidate, or less likely, or wouldn't it make any difference to you?"

It is apparent from Table VI-8 that at the time of our survey Senator McCarthy was not popular with any of the party identification groups. Only the strong Republicans gave our question about equal positive and negative responses.

Table VI-8

RELATION OF PARTY IDENTIFICATION TO ATTITUDE
TOWARD McCARTHY

"If you knew that Senator McCarthy was supporting a candidate for Congress, would you be more likely to vote for that candidate, or less likely, or wouldn't it make any difference to you?"

	Strong Democrat	Weak Democrat	Independent Democrat	Independent	Independent Republican	Weak Republican	Strong Republican
More likely to vote for candidate	8%	8%	6%	10%	10%	10%	22%
No vote effect, but pro-McCarthy	2	1	2	2	2	2	3
No vote effect— neutral toward McCarthy	37	44	42	54	50	47	43
No vote effect, but anti-McCarthy	4	4	3	1	--	3	1
Less likely to vote for candidate	46	36	38	20	32	30	26
Other responses	3	7	9	13	6	8	5
	100%	100%	100%	100%	100%	100%	100%
Number of cases	248	288	97	82	68	159	146

The distribution of responses in Table VI-8 follows the pattern we would expect to characterize a partisan issue. Strong Democrats were most disapproving; strong Republicans were most approving, with the other party groups graded roughly between these extremes. As we have stated earlier, ordinarily we would expect reactions to prominent party figures to follow partisan lines. It must be noted, however, that party differences are not as large in these responses to Senator McCarthy as they were to Mr. Eisenhower. There appear to be two reasons why this is the case:

• While Senator McCarthy was indubitably a Republican and must have been seen as such by our respondents, at the time of our study he was embroiled in a loud conflict with the leadership of his own party. The fact that many Republicans were pained by his performance is demonstrated in Table VI-2. Many of them must have found it difficult to support a senator whose loyalty to the party was as much in doubt as Senator McCarthy's was at that time.

• On the Democratic side reaction to the Senator was complicated for many good party followers by the fact that he was a fellow-Catholic. We find that Catholic Democrats were as a group much more favorable to Senator McCarthy than Protestant Democrats (Table B-81). This is a classic example of the effect of conflict in group memberships on political attitudes. Where group memberships were congruent (Protestant Democrats, Catholic Republicans) reactions to the Senator were most extreme. The conflicted Catholic Democrats fell between these two groups, with the result that the total Democratic assessment of the Senator was not as partisan as might have been expected.

Summary

The most evident conclusion to be drawn from Chapter VI is that Republicans and Democrats not only vote the party line; within limits they also think the party line. And people who call themselves "strong" Republicans or Democrats are consistently more likely than "weak" party followers to take a partisan position not only in voting but also on issues.

It is important to observe that these party differences in attitudes are not simply reflections of socio-economic differences in the make-up of the following of the two parties. There are significant differences between socio-economic groups in their attitudes on some of these issues (as we saw in Chapter IV) but the differences between party identifiers within each group tend to be greater than the differences between the groups themselves. Consider the following figures showing the proportions of strong party identifiers saying a Democratic or Republican victory would be financially better for them:

	Better off if Democrats win		Better off if Republicans win	
	Strong Republicans	Strong Democrats	Strong Republicans	Strong Democrats
Income less than $3000	4%	50%	30%	3%
$3000 to $6000	--%	57%	33%	5%
Over $6000	7%	42%	46%	5%

Reading the figures horizontally we see that the differences between adherents of the two parties who fall in the same income category are very large. Reading vertically, the differences between adherents of the same party who have different incomes are relatively small. The implication of these data is that while having a high or low income is influential in respect to one's feeling as to which party is best for him financially, being a Republican or Democrat also has an influence which is quite independent of income and considerably more important.

This picture characterizes nearly all of the questions we have considered. The variations between Democrats and Republicans of similar socio-economic characteristics are larger than the variations between Republicans (or Democrats) of different socio-economic groups. In the case of attitudes toward Senator McCarthy the pattern holds except when Protestants and Catholics are compared; religious and party differences are both strongly correlated with attitudes in this table.

In general our data conform to our expectation that differences between adherents of the two parties would be greatest when the issue considered was most clearly party-connected. The President himself epitomized the Republican party and we would expect party differences in evaluation of him to be large, as indeed they were. The fact that they were not larger probably reflects the generally favorable image of Mr. Eisenhower which many people of both parties apparently held at the time of this survey.

The question as to the financial consequences of a Republican or Democratic victory placed the party conflict in clear focus and the differences between the two groups of partisans were pronounced. Partisan differences in answers to the question regarding Senator McCarthy were less sharp than we would have predicted solely on the basis of his highly visible association with the Republican party. As we have seen, however, this question was complicated by other considerations which dulled the purely partisan edge of the McCarthy issue.

The only question for which party identification seems to have no significance while socio-economic position does is that dealing with foreign policy. As we have seen, Republicans and Democrats did not differ in their feeling as to whether this country had "gone too far" in its foreign involvements and they did not differ within the major socio-economic groups. Within the limits of our data we must conclude that foreign policy was not a partisan issue among the electorate in October 1954. It is important to observe that in 1954 the national leaderships of the two parties did not differ significantly in their positions regarding foreign policy.

These data regarding foreign policy attitudes do more than simply support our hypothesis regarding the correspondence between the partisan character of issues and partisan differences in public response to them. They also relate to the question of whether or not the leaders of the political parties, through the public positions they take, in fact shape the opinions of the people who identify with those parties. As we have seen, party identification is associated with political attitudes in ways which cannot be derived from socio-economic factors. This strongly suggests that party identification itself exerts pressure on the individual to conform to what he sees as party standards. We have not eliminated the possibility, however, that Republican identifiers hold Republican attitudes because they held the attitudes first (for unknown reasons) and identified themselves later with the Republican party when they saw that its position was similar to their own. In other words the party may serve an instrumental function rather than one of standard setting.

A review of the Survey Research Center's previous use of this question regarding foreign involvement reveals that Republicans and Democrats did not differ significantly in 1948 during the period of the bi-partisan foreign policy but in 1952 during the Korean war they differed substantially. Now in 1954 we find them very similar again and the change from the 1952 position is entirely accounted for by a shift among Republican adherents toward a more internationalist position.

It may be argued that the Republican shift merely reflects an unwillingness of Republicans to criticize foreign policy as long as their own party is responsible for it. Following this argument we should expect a compensating increase of criticism among Democrats, an increase which we do not find. We also find it hard to believe that the Republican change can be understood as part of a general public reaction to the end of the Korean war since Democrats did not change between 1952 and 1954.

95

The effective cause of the change among Republican identifiers appears to have been the strongly internationalist position
taken by the Eisenhower administration when it took office in
1953. Since we know from our earlier studies that there is
relatively little shifting from party to party over short periods
of time, there is a strong implication that the Eisenhower
leadership of the Republican party brought about a significant
shift in the foreign policy attitudes (insofar as we measured
them) of the Republican rank and file during the first two years
of its tenure.

These data do not give us the final word as to party identification as a force in political behavior. They certainly make
clear that the political label people give themselves in national
politics is much more than a name. As in most research in
the social sciences, it will be difficult to disentangle the various
influences to which the citizen reacts.

We have seen that socio-economic position and religious
and racial memberships can have political effects in specific
circumstances. Party identification seems to have implications
broader than most of the factors we have considered. The
sense of belonging to a party, which is held so widely in the
American electorate, is clearly a factor of the greatest interest
both to the practitioners of politics and to its academic students.

VII

DISCUSSION AND SUMMARY

We have not been surprised to discover that our data demonstrate sizeable differences in the political attitudes and votes of the major population groups that make up the American electorate. More interesting are the general conclusions which our study suggests regarding the interaction of group membership and political behavior.

We began our analysis with the assumption that a group position in the area of politics might come about either through coincidental but independent responses of individual members to outside stimuli or through the influence of the group itself on its membership. We have proposed that group individuality in voting and attitudes will be greatest when membership identification and group standards regarding political behavior are strongest. We do not expect to find group individuality when either or both of these properties is missing except in situations in which coincidental consensus results from the influence of some outside stimulus.

We do not have any direct measure in the study which will permit us to order the population groups we are considering in respect to the strength of the pressure they exert on the political behavior of their members. On the basis of general information regarding these groups, it is possible, however, to make an impressionistic estimate as to how they compare on this dimension.

We would not expect, for example, the sex and age groupings to stand high on such a scale. Both are extremely heterogeneous; neither is subject to outside pressures which might induce group solidarity. Men and women in particular are not differentiated politically. Since the end of the suffragette period, men and women have not had a history of separate platforms or separate media of information. The fact that most men and women live in family groups, with their strong pressure for political uniformity, militates against the development of independent and contrasting political movements based on sex differences. As we have seen, men and women did not demonstrate political individuality in the present study. In other words, men and women did not give any significant evidence of thinking and voting as men or women *per se*. Their votes and attitudes were determined by other considerations.[1]

Most of what we have said about sex groups also applies to age groups. In this country's recent history the only significant political movement associated with age was the Townsend Plan, a depression-born scheme of old-age pensions. Political activities among youth, prominent in other contemporary societies, are notably unimportant in the United States. Aside from a possible feeling that political radicalism is more becoming to youth than it is to age, we have no accepted standards of political behavior for the different age groups. American politics have not been organized around considerations of age.

Our comparison of the age groups showed us that they differed very little in their opinions on issues. The one apparent difference—a greater interest in social security among older people—appears to be a clear example of coincidental reaction to a common outside stimulus. The age groups do shift gradually in their voting preferences. Whether this results from changes during the life-cycle of individual voters or from a long-term shift toward the Democratic party among younger voters we do not know.

Life-cycle changes might reflect increased status and increased attraction to the "respectability" of the Republican party. A long-term shift presumably could be brought about by some national crisis which changed the public image of the two parties and swung the support of the younger, least committed part of the electorate from one party to the other. Whichever explanation is correct, the effects are not very pronounced and appear to be entirely at the level of party preferences rather than attitudes regarding issues.

---

1. Duverger summarizes a study of voting in several European countries with the following statement "There is nothing here to suggest an essential peculiarity in woman's nature or a fundamental difference in men's and women's behaviour." Duverger, M. , *The Political Role of Women*, Unesco, Paris, 1955.

In contrast to the sex and age groups we would expect the minority religious and racial groups to have a relatively high potential for influence on their members. These are groups in which membership is a highly conscious experience. They have a history of discrimination, they are segregated from some aspects of majority society, their members share many aspects of a minority culture. If we consider Jews and Negroes as the most distinct of the minority groups, we find an interesting contrast. Jews were one of the most individual of any of the groups we have considered, not only in their votes but in their issue positions. Their responses gave clear evidence of a patterned political orientation. Negroes, on the other hand, while showing a strong preference in their votes, revealed no strong group position on issues.

In view of recent world history it is hardly surprising to find American Jews a highly politicized group. The events of the last thirty years could hardly fail to impress the most obtuse with the political character of the "Jewish question." Less dramatically, the growing pressure in this country for legislation to prevent discrimination in employment and housing also has highlighted the political implications of Jewish group membership.

Along with this high group-awareness goes a strong pattern of group values. Not only are there contemporary issues on which strong group standards exist—for example, the defense of the state of Israel—but also, as Fuchs points out, there are traditional values in Jewish culture which have application in current affairs. The Jewish group combines high membership-identification with strong standards regarding political behavior and, as our meager data show, it is highly distinctive in its political characteristics.

The failure of our Negro sample to display any strong position on the issues we presented in our survey appears to derive from an absence of group standards regarding these issues and a relatively low sensitivity to the personal implications of political events. While for historical and other reasons the Negro minority appears in some respects to be less cohesive than the Jewish group, the critical difference seems to lie in the substantial difference in the political sophistication of the two groups. Negroes as a group are far less politically involved, no doubt the result of their underprivileged educational and economic situation and of the various devices employed very widely to discourage their political activity. As our data have shown, large proportions of our Negro respondents did not vote and had

99

no opinions on political issues. As Negroes have been drawn
into the political community, particularly in the Northern cities,
they have swung strongly to the Democratic party. This conversion of the Negro vote during the Roosevelt era, as we have
said, may have been the product of both individual decisions
and growing group pressure. Such influence as Negro group
membership may have, however, does not seem to extend beyond the vote itself and even there is not sufficient to stimulate
more than a very low rate of turnout.

We regard Catholics as a group of relatively high membership identification. While Catholics are not as visible or as
subject to minority group treatment as either Jews or Negroes,
the fact of being Catholic undoubtedly has great significance for
many people. We find that Catholics were clearly partisan in
their vote but not in their attitudes except when the questions
dealt with their co-religionist, Senator McCarthy. As we have
observed earlier, we do not know whether this latter response
resulted from purely individual reactions to a situation which
stimulated many Catholics similarly or whether it resulted from
group influence. Although there is reason to believe that this
group does conform to group standards on some political questions—as, for example, birth control legislation—there is no
reason to believe that Catholic standards were present for most
of the issues we considered and our study does not show a general political "line" among Catholics.[1]

Labor unions differ from the other groups we have considered in their formal organizational qualities, membership
dues, elected officers and parliamentary procedure. They are
also characterized by a rather vocal national leadership which
has increasingly attempted to educate the rank-and-file membership to a union point of view regarding politics. Labor
unions may be said to have relatively high membership identification and relatively clear group standards regarding voting and
certain political issues. As we have seen, labor union members are in fact quite different from non-members of similar
occupational status in their voting preferences; they also differ,
though less markedly, in their responses to the "bread and
butter" issues which were presented in the survey. All of these
differences were in the direction of the prescribed union norms.
They did not differ, however, in the area in which there is no
clear union standard, foreign affairs.

---

1. This presents an interesting conflict with earlier data reported by
Allinsmith, W. and B., Religious Affiliation and Politico-economic Attitude, *Public Opinion Quarterly*, 1948, *12*, 377-389.

Approximately one person in six of the adult population of this country has attended college. These people are not organized as union members are organized; neither are they socially isolated as minority groups tend to be. There is no national body to which they belong and there are no visible signs by which they can be readily identified. There has never been a significant political movement which appealed specifically to them. On the other hand, college people have more in common than many of the groups we have considered. They share the very important attribute of social and economic advantage. Perhaps more than any other single consideration, formal education serves to distinguish the social classes of American society. College training is clearly associated both objectively and subjectively[1] with superior status.

We are not in a position to say whether the distinctive pattern of attitudes which characterizes the college group comes from their common economic and experiential background or from an inclination to conform to what they see to be the political position of their "kind of people." We know from our 1952 study[2] that upper-middle-class people tended strongly to see the middle class as voting Republican in that election. There are indications from the present study that Democrats of the college level were under some pressure to draw away from their own party. It would be of great interest to explore more fully the possibility that an upper-status position, not only in votes but in political attitudes, has developed in this country and serves as a guide for people of upper-status standing or aspiration.[3]

The political individuality of what we have called the party identification groups is the most striking of any of the population categories we have considered. People who call themselves "Republicans" and "Democrats" are not only substantially different in their voting; they also differ markedly in their attitudes, particularly on those issues which are most obviously party-related. We also have limited evidence that as the party position changes on a prominent issue, the position of the party

---

1. We know from our earlier studies that self-estimates of social class are very highly correlated with years of formal education.
2. See *The Voter Decides*, page 214.
3. A different view of the political implications of status and class is advanced by R. Hofstadter in the "The Pseudo-Conservative Revolt," *American Scholar*, *24*, 1954. The hostile attitudes of the status-anxious people he describes contrast sharply with the positions taken by the high status college people in our survey.

adherents also changes. It is clear that these attitudes, changes in attitudes, and behaviors are most partisan among those people who are most strongly party-identified. All of these findings support the conclusion that the political parties exert a strong influence on the political characteristics of their followers.

The nature of party identification as a phenomenon of group membership has not been studied as thoroughly as some of the other group affiliations we have considered. We have a number of indications from our 1952 study, however, that party attachment is a much stronger psychological force than it is sometimes considered. We know, for example, that most party adherents hold to the same party as their parents, that most people have never thought of themselves as belonging to a party other than their present one, that most people associate with friends whom they see as supporting the same party they do. Party identification appears to be a stable and persistent trait. Its strength is impressively demonstrated when we compare the votes and attitudes of the party groups within subdivisions of the other groups—economic, educational, community, etc. As we have seen, it is the party variable which contributes the greatest share of the variance of the political measures.

The fact that party membership is more closely associated with votes and attitudes than the other group memberships we have considered reflects not only the strength of party identification but also the clarity of party standards regarding political thought and action. Uniquely among the various population groups, the parties are characterized by clear prescriptions to guide the political activities of their followers. No Republican or Democrat is likely to find himself uncertain as to how his party feels he should vote in any particular election. If he keeps himself politically informed he also knows where his party stands on the major issues. More than any other population group, the parties, through the pronouncements of their spokesmen, provide structure in that area of the cognitive map that has to do with politics.

In considering the psychological functions which group memberships serve it seems apparent that each of the population groups we have considered has its own special relevance. While dividing the population into men and women provides us little insight into the explanation of political behavior, it would have important implications in the realm of manners and taste. Knowing that a person is a Protestant or a Catholic tells us a great deal more about his religious beliefs than it does about his politics. Being a Negro, a labor union member, a farmer, a college graduate, or a suburbanite all have special relevance which we would expect to find reflected in the appropriate areas of attitudes and values. The relevance of being a Republican or a Democrat is specifically political. While knowledge of this particular group membership would not help us understand religious, economic, artistic or many other types of beliefs and acts, it is essential for an understanding of political behavior.

It is apparent that our speculations regarding the solidarity of these various groups and the amount of pressure they exert on their members do not provide the basis for an adequate test of our hypothesis regarding group differences. We lack an effective measure of the group properties with which we are concerned. Within the present data we cannot properly go beyond the statement that the political characteristics of the groups we have studied appear to relate meaningfully to our impressionistic estimate of their membership identification and group standards.

If high membership identification and strong group standards are associated with group individuality as we have proposed, it should follow that within such a group those individuals who are most strongly group-identified will conform most closely to the standards of the group. Our data permit us to apply this hypothesis only in respect to party identification. As we have seen, in their voting and attitudes the party groups conform almost without exception to our expectation.

One amendment to this hypothesis needs to be considered, even though it cannot be fully tested within our present data. Just as we expect a group of high membership identification to show the strongest group positions in areas in which it has the strongest group standards, so we expect a highly identified group member to conform most closely to those group standards of which he is most acutely aware.

Thus we were able to demonstrate in our 1951 study of party identification and attitudes regarding foreign policy that well-informed party followers were much more likely to conform to their party's position on foreign affairs than were poorly informed. Our conclusion was that the well-informed found it easy to follow their party because they knew what its position was, while the poorly informed were less sure of their party's position and so less influenced by it. Consistent with this is the finding in the present report that the party identification groups are most partisan on those issues on which party lines are most clearly drawn.

103

Conformity to group standards is not always a highly conscious process, of course. No doubt many good Democrats and Republicans faithfully follow their party's position in the firm conviction that their opinions are entirely independent of any party influence. It is easily possible for a person to take on the peculiar coloration of his social group by a largely unconscious absorption of the values and standards of the people around him. Standards must exist if there is to be group conformity, but the individual group member may be influenced in ways of which he is not explicitly aware.

It is regrettable that our study did not inquire into the strength of the identification our respondents felt regarding some of the other population groups to which they belonged. Developing valid measures of strength of group belonging presents difficulties, but even such a crude dichotomy of "strong" and "weak" as we employed in our party identification scale would have been useful. It would be particularly interesting to examine the political implications of degrees of identification with the religious and labor union groups. The available data on this question are rather ambiguous. The Berelson study of Elmira reported virtually no difference between the votes of Catholics who rated their church as one of their most important organizations and those who did not. Our 1952 study found a small difference in the expected direction between Catholics of regular and infrequent church attendance. Berelson found some difference in partisanship among Jews who considered their religious identification most important or not so important. Fuchs, however, does not confirm this finding. Berelson also found a modest difference, although less than one might have anticipated, in the votes of union members who regarded their union as among their most important organizations and of those who did not. Further study of this problem is clearly desirable.

The fact that every member of the American electorate is simultaneously a member of numerous population groups means that many people are subject to political influence from more than one group. These influences may be either reinforcing or conflicting. It is our hypothesis that if these group influences are congruent those people holding overlapping position will be more partisan in their votes and attitudes than people who belong to only one of these relevant groups, and if these group influences are in conflict they will be less partisan. There are a number of tests of this hypothesis in the tables we have presented and in general the data conform to our expectations.

These comparisons of overlapping groups also provide a basis of estimating the relative importance of the political influence of different group memberships. We see, for example, that union members hold very steadily to a Democratic preference in their votes regardless of differences in income, education, or location, while non-members vary systemically with all three of these factors. On the other hand, union members who identify with the Republican party are just as solid in their vote for Republican candidates as are non-members who identify themselves as Republicans.

Our analysis of the effects of overlap in group memberships would be very much more satisfying if we knew more than the simple fact that our respondents fell inside or outside of a particular group. As we have observed, our data are deficient in not telling us whether the people we have classified in the different population groups actually identified themselves with those groups. This leaves us wondering, for example, whether the Republican union members we have just referred to were in fact union members "in name only." The fact that their voting behavior exhibits no evidence of conflict between union and party pressures would appear to contradict our hypothesis regarding the effects of overlapping membership. This contradiction is resolved, however, if these people did not identify themselves with their union since we do not expect to find a need to conform to group standards among people who are not group-identified.

A number of further explorations of the role of groups in the determination of political attitudes and votes are suggested by the present study. Not only do we need measures of individual identification with groups; it would also be desirable to have measures of the presence and strength of group pressure. Fuller information regarding the image members have of the groups to which they belong and of those to which they do not belong would make possible a more specific analysis of the conditions associated with conformity and lack of conformity. Further examples of changes in group standards should be sought, since they provide particular insight into the nature of group effects. Similarly the reorientation of attitudes and perceptions that occurs when an individual shifts his allegiance from one group to another offers research opportunities of great interest.[1] All of these inquiries were beyond the scope of the present study but they are not beyond the range of fruitful investigation by students of group phenomena.

---

1. For example, see Seymour Lieberman's "The Effects of Changes in Role on the Attitudes of Role Occupants," to appear in *Human Relations*.

Summary

The study presented in this report was undertaken with two major objectives—to bring forward to 1954 the Survey Research Center series of quantitative descriptions of the national elections, and to expand our understanding of the relation of the individual citizen's group attachments to his political attitudes and behavior. While limitations on the scope of the study severely restricted the analysis which could be carried out, the data collected were adequate to support the following summary statements:

1. Group differences in attitudes and votes clearly exist. Although they are substantial and persistent they are not exclusive. No population category (except the party identification groups) fails to show a significant minority who dissent from the prevailing group position.

2. Some group differences appear to be brought about by similar but independent reactions of individual members to commonly perceived outside stimuli. Others appear to result from conformity to perceived group standards.

3. Group differences are greater in votes than in attitudes. However, votes and attitudes are related. Groups that support one party in their votes tend to support that party's position on partisan issues.

4. Differences in turnout are found between people who identify with the Republican and Democratic parties which cannot be explained on the basis of socio-economic differences. Personal characteristics underlying turnout are suggested.

5. Most groups do not have an integrated pattern of political attitudes that distinguishes them from other groups. Many groups react in an individual way to specific issues but broad patterns of response are found only in the most homogeneous and sophisticated groups.

6. Political party identification is more closely associated with the vote than is any of the other population variables. The relationship is stronger with the partisanship of the vote than it is with the turnout.

7. Party identification is meaningfully associated with attitudes on issues which are clearly party-related; it is

not associated with attitudes on issues which are not party-related. Party-identification groups differ more widely in attitudes on party-related issues than do the other population groups.

8. There is evidence that change in the position of party leadership regarding political issues produces change in the attitudes of those identified with the party.

9. Strength of party identification is associated with conformity to party standards both in voting and in attitudes regarding issues.

10. Political individuality is most marked in those groups which appear to have high membership identification and strong group standards relating to politics.

11. Overlapping group membership tends to accentuate political individuality if the political orientations of the overlapping groups are congruent; it tends to diminish it if they are in conflict.

APPENDIX

APPENDIX   A

Sample Design and Sampling Errors[1]

The individuals interviewed in this survey are a representative cross-section of citizens of voting age living in private households in the United States.   Since the survey was restricted to private households, those people residing in military establishments, hospitals, religious and educational institutions, logging and lumber camps, penal institutions, hotels, and larger rooming houses were excluded from the sample.   These excluded groups, which comprise very roughly about five percent of the adult population of the United States, were omitted from the defined population because the usual sampling procedures would cause serious practical difficulties when applied to these groups, and because a large proportion of these people are legally or otherwise disfranchised.   The sample was selected by a probability method with procedures known as area sampling. By this method every member of the population sampled had a known chance of being selected.

Survey results are subject to two major kinds of error. First, there are whatever inaccuracies occur in the respondents' answers and in the way they are recorded by the interviewers—the so-called "reporting" errors including non-response.   In most cases the magnitude of these errors can only be surmised. Another type of error is called sampling error.   It results from the fact that the survey is based upon a sample rather than upon interviews with the entire population.   There is always the possibility that by chance the sample will contain too many or too few Republicans, too many or too few people who believe foreign involvement is undesirable, etc.

The sampling error measures the limits on either side of the obtained figures within which the true population value has a given probability of falling.   It is customary to give, as "the

---

1. Adapted from *The Voter Decides.*

sampling error," a figure representing two standard errors; this represents the limits within which the true value will lie 95 out of 100 times.

The sampling error varies somewhat for the different findings of the survey. Despite these differences, tables representing the approximate magnitudes of the sampling errors of various estimated percentages will give a general picture of the degree of variability that should be attached to the estimates. Tables A-1 and A-2 represent a generalized compromise result. However, the sampling error for any particular item may in fact be one percentage point lower or higher than that given in the tables.

Table A-1 may be used to determine the sampling error for the difference of two proportions when comparing two subgroups, both of which are based on all sample points. The Ns of the two subgroups and the average size of the two proportions being compared are necessary for entering the table. If, for example, the two groups being compared were based on Ns of 200 and 500 respectively, the proper "box" in the table is found in the row marked N=500 and the column marked N=200. Where the proportions being compared are about 50 percent, the sampling error is about 10 percent; where the proportions being compared are about 20 percent, the sampling error is about 8 percent; etc.

Table A-2 may be used to determine the sampling error for estimated proportions of groups based on all sample points. The size of the group and the size of the proportion being estimated are needed for entering the table. If, for example, the size of the group is 300, then the proper "box" is found in the column marked N=300. Proportions around 50 percent have a sampling error of about 7 percent; proportions around 20 percent have a sampling error of about 6 percent; etc. Thus, if a proportion based on an N=300 were estimated to be 45 percent, then the true population value has a 95 percent probability of falling within the range 45-7 percent and 45+7 percent--thus, between 38 and 52 percent.

Table A-1

SAMPLING ERRORS OF DIFFERENCES

Differences required for significance (95 percent probability) in comparisons of percentages based on two successive surveys or on different subgroups of the sample.

Size of sample or subgroup	Size of sample or subgroup					
	1000	500	300	200	100	40
For percentages between 35% and 65%:						
1000	7	7	8	9	11	17
500		8	9	10	12	17
300			10	10	12	17
200				11	13	18
100					15	19
40						23
For percentages near 20% or 80%:						
1000	6	6	7	8	9	13
500		7	7	8	9	14
300			8	9	10	14
200				9	10	14
100					12	15
40						18
For percentages near 10% or 90%:						
1000	4	5	5	6	7	--
500		5	5	6	7	--
300			6	6	7	--
200				7	8	--
100					9	--

113

Table A-2

SAMPLING ERRORS OF REPORTED PERCENTAGES

The chances are 95 in 100 that the reported sample value does not differ from the population value by more than the number of percentage points shown below.

Reported percentage	Number of interviews on which the percentage is based					
	1000	500	300	200	100	40
From 35% to 65%	5	6	7	8	11	16
Near 20% or 80%	4	5	6	7	9	13
Near 10% or 90%	3	4	4	5	7	--
Near 5% or 95%	2	3	3	4	--	--

APPENDIX B

Tables Referred to in the Text

Table B-1

RELATION OF EDUCATION TO PROBABLE 1954 VOTE WITHIN INCOME GROUPS

	Less than $3000			$3,000 to $6,000			More than $6,000		
	Grade school	High school	College	Grade school	High school	College	Grade school	High school	College
Probable vote:									
Democratic	19%	24%	24%	28%	26%	26%	17%	22%	25%
Republican	13	20	24	18	19	34	28	35	37
Probable non-voter	68	56	52	54	55	40	55	43	38
	100%	100%	100%	100%	100%	100%	100%	100%	100%
Number of cases	226	118	21	141	265	82	36	113	91

114

Table B-2

RELATION OF EDUCATION TO PROBABLE 1954 VOTE AMONG UNION MEMBERS AND NON-MEMBERS

	Members			Non-members		
	Grade school	High school	College	Grade school	High school	College
Probable vote:						
Democratic	29%	33%	38%	20%	20%	23%
Republican	13	20	21	17	23	37
Probable non-voter	58	47	41	63	57	40
	100%	100%	100%	100%	100%	100%
Number of cases	110	177	29	298	335	172

Table B-3

RELATION OF EDUCATION TO PROBABLE 1954 VOTE WITHIN TYPES OF COMMUNITY

	Metropolitan			City or town			Open country		
	Grade school	High school	College	Grade school	High school	College	Grade school	High school	College
Probable vote:									
Democratic	25%	24%	22%	23%	27%	25%	19%	18%	29%
Republican	20	21	42	16	25	33	13	16	24
Probable non-voter	55	55	36	61	48	42	68	66	47
	100%	100%	100%	100%	100%	100%	100%	100%	100%
Number of cases	73	178	67	221	263	114	122	76	21

RELATION OF LABOR UNION AFFILIATION TO PROBABLE
1954 VOTE WITHIN TYPES OF COMMUNITY

	Metropolitan		City or town		Open country	
	Member	Non-member	Member	Non-member	Member	Non-member
Probable vote:						
Democratic	35%	18%	32%	23%	24%	19%
Republican	19	29	18	25	15	15
Probable non-voter	46	53	50	52	61	66
	100%	100%	100%	100%	100%	100%
Number of cases	107	209	176	415	33	184

Table B-5

RELATION OF LABOR UNION AFFILIATION TO PROBABLE 1954 VOTE
WITHIN INCOME GROUPS

	Less than $3000		$3000 to $6000		More than $6000	
	Member	Non-member	Member	Non-member	Member	Non-member
Probable vote:						
Democratic	27%	19%	35%	22%	29%	20%
Republican	24	15	14	26	25	39
Probable non-voter	49	66	51	52	46	41
	100%	100%	100%	100%	100%	100%
Number of cases	49	311	196	290	65	173

116

Table B-6

OPINIONS OF MEN AND WOMEN AS TO THE "BEST THING THE REPUBLICANS HAVE DONE"

	Men	Women	Total
Ended the Korean war	29%	26%	28%
Reduced taxes	8	8	7
Reduced governmental expenditures	7	5	6
Extended social security	5	5	5
Got Communists out of government	3	3	3
Desegregated schools	2	3	3
Other	18	12	15
Don't know	20	33	27
Everything bad	8	5	6
	100%	100%	100%
Number of cases	532	607	1139

Table B-7

RELATION OF AGE TO THE "BEST THING THE REPUBLICANS HAVE DONE"

	21-34	35-54	Over 55
Ended the Korean war	27%	28%	27%
Reduced taxes	9	8	6
Reduced governmental expenditures	5	7	4
Extended social security	4	5	9
Got Communists out of government	2	3	3
Desegregated schools	4	2	3
Other	16	14	15
Don't know	27	27	27
Everything bad	6	6	6
	100%	100%	100%
Number of cases	366	485	281

Table B-8

RELATION OF RELIGION TO THE "BEST THING
THE REPUBLICANS HAVE DONE"

	Protestant	Catholic	Jewish
Ended the Korean war	29%	27%	9%
Reduced taxes	7	9	15
Reduced governmental expenditures	6	4	3
Extended social security	5	7	20
Got Communists out of government	3	3	--
Desegregated schools	3	1	9
Other	15	13	20
Don't know	28	28	12
Everything bad	4	8	12
	100%	100%	100%
Number of cases	857	217	34

Table B-9

RELATION OF RACE TO THE "BEST THING
THE REPUBLICANS HAVE DONE"

	White	Negro
Ended the Korean war	28%	18%
Reduced taxes	8	4
Reduced governmental expenditures	7	1
Extended social security	6	3
Got Communists out of government	3	1
Desegregated schools	2	12
Other	16	8
Don't know	24	45
Everything bad	6	8
	100%	100%
Number of cases	1022	103

Table B-10

RELATION OF SIZE OF COMMUNITY TO
THE "BEST THING THE REPUBLICANS HAVE DONE"

	Metro centers	Metro suburbs	City or town	Open country
Ended the Korean war	17%	29%	30%	29%
Reduced taxes	12	8	6	6
Reduced governmental expenditures	4	6	6	6
Extended social security	12	3	5	2
Got Communists out of government	2	5	2	4
Desegregated schools	5	4	2	1
Other	15	17	16	12
Don't know	28	22	26	35
Everything bad	5	6	7	5
	100%	100%	100%	100%
Number of cases	169	150	601	219

Table B-11

RELATION OF EDUCATION TO
THE "BEST THING THE REPUBLICANS HAVE DONE"

	Grade school	High school	College
Ended the Korean war	27%	29%	25%
Reduced taxes	4	9	8
Reduced governmental expenditures	2	6	13
Extended social security	6	6	4
Got Communists out of government	3	3	2
Desegregated schools	2	3	4
Other	11	13	30
Don't know	38	25	10
Everything bad	7	6	4
	100%	100%	100%
Number of cases	416	517	202

119

Table B-12

RELATION OF OCCUPATION OF FAMILY HEAD TO
THE "BEST THING THE REPUBLICANS HAVE DONE"

	Professional, business	Clerical, sales	Skilled labor	Unskilled labor	Farm operators
Ended the Korean war	25%	30%	28%	24%	39%
Reduced taxes	10	6	8	10	3
Reduced governmental expenditures	11	11	4	4	4
Extended social security	5	5	7	3	1
Got Communists out of government	3	5	2	3	2
Desegregated schools	2	--	3	3	--
Other	23	25	10	11	12
Don't know	17	13	30	35	31
Everything bad	4	5	8	7	8
	100%	100%	100%	100%	100%
Number of cases	246	102	337	144	104

Table B-13

RELATION OF LABOR UNION AFFILIATION TO
THE "BEST THING THE REPUBLICANS HAVE DONE"

	Total population		Laborers only	
	Union member	Non-member	Union member	Non-member
Ended the Korean war	31%	26%	33%	22%
Reduced taxes	7	8	8	9
Reduced governmental expenditures	5	6	4	3
Extended social security	7	5	6	6
Got Communists out of government	2	3	1	3
Desegregated schools	5	2	4	1
Other	10	17	8	13
Don't know	24	28	26	39
Everything bad	9	5	10	4
	100%	100%	100%	100%
Number of cases	316	808	240	235

Table B-14

RELATION OF INCOME TO THE
"BEST THING THE REPUBLICANS HAVE DONE"

	Under $3000	$3000-6000	Over $6000
Ended the Korean war	26%	32%	20%
Reduced taxes	5	8	9
Reduced governmental expenditures	2	6	11
Extended social security	5	5	7
Got Communists out of government	2	4	2
Desegregated schools	3	2	4
Other	11	14	24
Don't know	40	22	18
Everything bad	6	7	5
	100%	100%	100%
Number of cases	367	489	240

Table B-15

OPINIONS OF MEN AND WOMEN AS TO THE
"WORST THING THE REPUBLICANS HAVE DONE"

	Men	Women	Total
Mishandled McCarthy	14%	12%	13%
Poor farm program	7	4	5
Unemployment	5	4	4
Poor tax program	5	3	4
Desegregated schools	3	4	4
Too lenient toward Russia	3	1	2
Other	23	17	19
Don't know	28	44	37
Everything good	12	11	12
	100%	100%	100%
Number of cases	532	607	1139

Table B-16

RELATION OF AGE TO THE
"WORST THING THE REPUBLICANS HAVE DONE"

	21-34	35-54	Over 55
Mishandled McCarthy	13%	14%	11%
Poor farm program	5	5	6
Unemployment	5	4	4
Poor tax program	2	5	5
Desegregated schools	6	3	1
Too lenient toward Russia	3	2	1
Other	19	20	20
Don't know	37	36	39
Everything good	10	11	13
	100%	100%	100%
Number of cases	366	485	281

Table B-17

RELATION OF RELIGION TO THE
"WORST THING THE REPUBLICANS HAVE DONE"

	Protestant	Catholic	Jewish
Mishandled McCarthy	13%	11%	21%
Poor farm program	5	5	3
Unemployment	4	5	--
Poor tax program	3	6	3
Desegregated schools	4	3	3
Too lenient toward Russia	2	5	3
Other	19	19	35
Don't know	38	34	23
Everything good	12	12	9
	100%	100%	100%
Number of cases	857	217	34

Table B-18

RELATION OF RACE TO THE
"WORST THING THE REPUBLICANS HAVE DONE"

	White	Negro
Mishandled McCarthy	13%	6%
Poor farm program	6	1
Unemployment	3	12
Poor tax program	4	3
Desegregated schools	3	5
Too lenient toward Russia	3	--
Other	20	15
Don't know	36	52
Everything good	12	6
	100%	100%
Number of cases	1022	103

Table B-19

RELATION OF SIZE OF COMMUNITY TO
THE "WORST THING THE REPUBLICANS HAVE DONE"

	Metro centers	Metro suburbs	City or town	Open country
Mishandled McCarthy	15%	20%	13%	5%
Poor farm program	2	2	4	15
Unemployment	2	7	4	5
Poor tax program	2	3	5	2
Desegregated schools	5	2	3	4
Too lenient toward Russia	4	2	2	2
Other	28	20	20	12
Don't know	34	33	35	47
Everything good	8	11	14	8
	100%	100%	100%	100%
Number of cases	169	150	601	219

Table B-20

RELATION OF EDUCATION TO THE "WORST THING THE REPUBLICANS HAVE DONE"

	Grade school	High school	College
Mishandled McCarthy	6%	13%	26%
Poor farm program	6	4	9
Unemployment	7	3	1
Poor tax program	5	3	4
Desegregated schools	3	4	3
Too lenient toward Russia	1	3	4
Other	14	23	23
Don't know	48	35	16
Everything good	10	12	14
	100%	100%	100%
Number of cases	416	517	202

Table B-21

RELATION OF OCCUPATION OF FAMILY HEAD TO THE "WORST THING THE REPUBLICANS HAVE DONE"

	Professional, business	Clerical, sales	Skilled labor	Unskilled labor	Farm operators
Mishandled McCarthy	23%	17%	9%	10%	5%
Poor farm program	6	4	3	4	19
Unemployment	1	4	5	9	2
Poor tax program	3	5	5	3	--
Desegregated schools	4	6	4	4	2
Too lenient toward Russia	2	6	2	2	2
Other	20	22	24	15	11
Don't know	28	23	37	42	50
Everything good	13	13	11	11	9
	100%	100%	100%	100%	100%
Number of cases	246	102	337	144	104

Table B-22

RELATION OF LABOR UNION AFFILIATION TO
THE "WORST THING THE REPUBLICANS HAVE DONE"

	Total population		Laborers only	
	Union member	Non-member	Union member	Non-member
Mishandled McCarthy	11%	13%	11%	8%
Poor farm program	3	6	3	4
Unemployment	8	3	8	4
Poor tax program	7	3	5	3
Desegregated schools	2	4	2	6
Too lenient toward Russia	3	2	3	2
Other	25	18	25	17
Don't know	31	39	32	45
Everything good	10	12	11	11
	100%	100%	100%	100%
Number of cases	316	808	240	235

Table B-23

RELATION OF INCOME TO THE
"WORST THING THE REPUBLICANS HAVE DONE"

	Under $3000	$3000-6000	Over $6000
Mishandled McCarthy	7%	11%	25%
Poor farm program	7	5	5
Unemployment	4	5	3
Poor tax program	4	3	6
Desegregated schools	4	4	3
Too lenient toward Russia	1	2	4
Other	14	23	19
Don't know	49	35	22
Everything good	10	12	13
	100%	100%	100%
Number of cases	367	489	240

Table B-24

SATISFACTION WITH EISENHOWER AMONG
MEN AND WOMEN

Eisenhower performance	Men	Women	Total
As good as or better than expected	64%	68%	66%
As expected, but didn't expect much	7	8	8
Expectations not fulfilled, but not disappointed	3	1	2
Disappointed	20	16	19
Other responses	6	7	5
	100%	100%	100%
Number of cases	532	607	1139

Table B-25

RELATION OF AGE TO SATISFACTION
WITH EISENHOWER

Eisenhower performance	21-34	35-54	Over 55
As good as or better than expected	63%	67%	67%
As expected, but didn't expect much	9	6	7
Expectations not fulfilled, but not disappointed	2	1	3
Disappointed	20	18	18
Other responses	6	8	5
	100%	100%	100%
Number of cases	366	485	281

126

Table B-26

RELATION OF RELIGION TO SATISFACTION WITH EISENHOWER

Eisenhower performance	Protestant	Catholic	Jewish
As good as or better than expected	68%	61%	50%
As expected, but didn't expect much	8	7	12
Expectations not fulfilled, but not disappointed	2	2	3
Disappointed	17	22	23
Other responses	5	8	12
	100%	100%	100%
Number of cases	857	217	34

Table B-27

RELATION OF RACE TO SATISFACTION WITH EISENHOWER

Eisenhower performance	White	Negro
As good as or better than expected	66%	61%
As expected, but didn't expect much	8	4
Expectations not fulfilled, but not disappointed	2	3
Disappointed	18	19
Other responses	6	13
	100%	100%
Number of cases	1022	103

Table B-28

RELATION OF SIZE OF COMMUNITY TO
SATISFACTION WITH EISENHOWER

Eisenhower performance	Metro centers	Metro suburbs	City or town	Open country
As good as or better than expected	57%	71%	65%	73%
As expected, but didn't expect much	9	5	7	8
Expectations not fulfilled, but not disappointed	3	1	2	2
Disappointed	22	19	19	13
Other responses	9	4	7	4
	100%	100%	100%	100%
Number of cases	169	150	601	219

Table B-29

RELATION OF EDUCATION TO SATISFACTION
WITH EISENHOWER

Eisenhower performance	Grade school	High school	College
As good as or better than expected	66%	67%	65%
As expected, but didn't expect much	7	8	7
Expectations not fulfilled, but not disappointed	2	1	2
Disappointed	16	18	23
Other responses	9	6	3
	100%	100%	100%
Number of cases	416	517	202

Table B-30

RELATION OF OCCUPATION OF FAMILY HEAD TO
SATISFACTION WITH EISENHOWER

Eisenhower performance	Professional, business	Clerical, sales	Skilled labor	Unskilled labor	Farm operators
As good as or better than expected	66%	75%	61%	62%	77%
As expected, but didn't expect much	8	4	10	7	7
Expectations not fulfilled, but not disappointed	2	1	2	3	2
Disappointed	20	17	20	16	12
Other responses	4	3	7	12	2
	100%	100%	100%	100%	100%
Number of cases	246	102	337	144	104

Table B-31

RELATION OF LABOR UNION AFFILIATION TO
SATISFACTION WITH EISENHOWER

Eisenhower performance	Total population		Laborers only	
	Union member	Non-member	Union member	Non-member
As good as or better than expected	59%	69%	58%	65%
As expected, but didn't expect much	11	6	13	5
Expectations not fulfilled, but not disappointed	2	2	2	2
Disappointed	22	16	20	18
Other responses	6	7	7	10
	100%	100%	100%	100%
Number of cases	316	808	240	235

Table B-32

RELATION OF INCOME TO SATISFACTION WITH EISENHOWER

Eisenhower performance	Under $3000	$3000-6000	Over $6000
As good as or better than expected	67%	64%	69%
As expected, but didn't expect much	6	9	8
Expectations not fulfilled, but not disappointed	1	2	2
Disappointed	16	20	17
Other responses	10	5	4
	100%	100%	100%
Number of cases	367	489	240

Table B-33

RATING OF EISENHOWER BY MEN AND WOMEN

	Men	Women	Total
Better than average	24%	22%	23%
Average	58	63	61
Poorer than average	12	7	10
Other responses	6	8	6
	100%	100%	100%
Number of cases	532	607	1139

Table B-34

RELATION OF AGE TO RATING OF EISENHOWER

	21-34	35-54	Over 55
Better than average	21%	21%	28%
Average	64	65	50
Poorer than average	11	8	11
Other responses	4	6	11
	100%	100%	100%
Number of cases	366	485	281

Table B-35

RELATION OF RELIGION TO RATING OF EISENHOWER

	Protestant	Catholic	Jewish
Better than average	24%	19%	21%
Average	62	62	47
Poorer than average	8	13	15
Other responses	6	6	17
	100%	100%	100%
Number of cases	857	217	34

Table B-36

RELATION OF RACE TO RATING OF EISENHOWER

	White	Negro
Better than average	24%	13%
Average	60	63
Poorer than average	9	17
Other responses	7	7
	100%	100%
Number of cases	1022	103

Table B-37

RELATION OF SIZE OF COMMUNITY
TO RATING OF EISENHOWER

	Metro centers	Metro suburbs	City or town	Open country
Better than average	22%	34%	22%	18%
Average	54	52	62	69
Poorer than average	14	8	10	6
Other responses	10	6	6	7
	100%	100%	100%	100%
Number of cases	169	150	601	219

Table B-38

RELATION OF EDUCATION TO RATING OF EISENHOWER

	Grade school	High school	College
Better than average	14%	24%	39%
Average	64	63	49
Poorer than average	12	9	7
Other responses	10	4	5
	100%	100%	100%
Number of cases	416	517	202

Table B-39

RELATION OF OCCUPATION OF FAMILY HEAD
TO RATING OF EISENHOWER

	Professional, business	Clerical, sales	Skilled labor	Unskilled labor	Farm operators
Better than average	33%	32%	16%	13%	19%
Average	53	60	66	68	70
Poorer than average	6	4	12	12	6
Other responses	8	4	6	7	5
	100%	100%	100%	100%	100%
Number of cases	246	102	337	144	104

132

Table B-40

RELATION OF LABOR UNION AFFILIATION TO RATING OF EISENHOWER

| | Total population | | Laborers only | |
	Union member	Non-member	Union member	Non-member
Better than average	17%	25%	15%	15%
Average	65	61	67	66
Poorer than average	13	8	13	12
Other responses	5	6	5	7
	100%	100%	100%	100%
Number of cases	316	808	240	235

Table B-41

RELATION OF INCOME TO RATING OF EISENHOWER

	Under $3000	$3000-6000	Over $6000
Better than average	19%	21%	32%
Average	61	63	57
Poorer than average	11	11	5
Other responses	9	5	6
	100%	100%	100%
Number of cases	367	489	240

Table B-42

EXPECTED EFFECT OF ELECTION OUTCOME ON PERSONAL FINANCES

"Do you think it will make any difference in how you and your family get along financially whether the Democrats or Republicans win?"

	October 1952	October 1954
Better off if Democrats win	29%	21%
Doesn't make any difference	45	59
Better off if Republicans win	15	12
Don't know	11	8
	100%	100%
Number of cases	1799	1139

Table B-43

EXPECTED EFFECT OF ELECTION OUTCOME ON PERSONAL FINANCES AMONG MEN AND WOMEN

	Men	Women
Better off if Democrats win	25%	20%
Doesn't make any difference	59	59
Better off if Republicans win	11	10
Don't know	5	11
	100%	100%
Number of cases	532	607

Table B-44

RELATION OF AGE TO EXPECTED EFFECT OF
ELECTION OUTCOME ON PERSONAL FINANCES

	21-34	35-54	Over 55
Better off if Democrats win	23%	22%	20%
Doesn't make any difference	59	58	60
Better off if Republicans win	9	12	12
Don't know	9	8	8
	100%	100%	100%
Number of cases	366	485	281

Table B-45

RELATION OF RELIGION TO EXPECTED EFFECT OF
ELECTION OUTCOME ON PERSONAL FINANCES

	Protestant	Catholic	Jewish
Better off if Democrats win	21%	22%	18%
Doesn't make any difference	59	62	65
Better off if Republicans win	11	10	15
Don't know	9	6	2
	100%	100%	100%
Number of cases	857	217	34

Table B-46

RELATION OF RACE TO EXPECTED EFFECT OF
ELECTION OUTCOME ON PERSONAL FINANCES

	White	Negro
Better off if Democrats win	20%	38%
Doesn't make any difference	61	37
Better off if Republicans win	12	4
Don't know	7	21
	100%	100%
Number of cases	1022	103

Table B-47

RELATION OF SIZE OF COMMUNITY TO EXPECTED
EFFECT OF ELECTION OUTCOME ON PERSONAL FINANCES

	Metro centers	Metro suburbs	City or town	Open country
Better off if Democrats win	27%	19%	21%	21%
Doesn't make any difference	54	63	60	58
Better off if Republicans win	12	16	10	8
Don't know	7	2	9	13
	100%	100%	100%	100%
Number of cases	169	150	601	219

Table B-48

RELATION OF EDUCATION TO EXPECTED EFFECT OF
ELECTION OUTCOME ON PERSONAL FINANCES

	Grade school	High school	College
Better off if Democrats win	25%	22%	14%
Doesn't make any difference	53	60	66
Better off if Republicans win	8	12	16
Don't know	14	6	4
	100%	100%	100%
Number of cases	416	517	202

Table B-49

RELATION OF OCCUPATION OF FAMILY HEAD TO EXPECTED EFFECT
OF ELECTION OUTCOME ON PERSONAL FINANCES

	Professional, business	Clerical, sales	Skilled labor	Unskilled labor	Farm operators
Better off if Democrats win	16%	14%	25%	29%	27%
Doesn't make any difference	63	66	58	52	53
Better off if Republicans win	14	16	10	7	9
Don't know	7	4	7	12	11
	100%	100%	100%	100%	100%
Number of cases	246	102	337	144	104

Table B-50

RELATION OF LABOR UNION AFFILIATION TO EXPECTED
EFFECT OF ELECTION OUTCOME ON PERSONAL FINANCES

	Total population		Laborers only	
	Union member	Non-member	Union member	Non-member
Better off if Democrats win	30%	18%	31%	22%
Doesn't make any difference	55	61	54	60
Better off if Republicans win	10	11	10	7
Don't know	5	10	5	11
	100%	100%	100%	100%
Number of cases	316	808	240	235

Table B-51

RELATION OF INCOME TO EXPECTED EFFECT OF
ELECTION OUTCOME ON PERSONAL FINANCES

	Under $3000	$3000-6000	Over $6000
Better off if Democrats win	24%	23%	17%
Doesn't make any difference	55	61	61
Better off if Republicans win	7	10	18
Don't know	14	6	4
	100%	100%	100%
Number of cases	367	489	240

Table B-52

ATTITUDES TOWARD U.S. INVOLVEMENT IN WORLD AFFAIRS
AMONG MEN AND WOMEN

	Men	Women
Too much involved	41%	42%
Pro-con, depends	2	4
Not too much involved	51	42
Other responses	6	12
	100%	100%
Number of cases	532	607

137

Table B-53

RELATION OF AGE TO U.S. INVOLVEMENT IN
WORLD AFFAIRS

	21-34	35-54	Over 55
Too much involved	41%	39%	49%
Pro-con, depends	3	3	2
Not too much involved	48	47	40
Other responses	8	11	9
	100%	100%	100%
Number of cases	366	485	281

Table B-54

RELATION OF RELIGION TO U.S. INVOLVEMENT IN
WORLD AFFAIRS

	Protestant	Catholic	Jewish
Too much involved	42%	44%	24%
Pro-con, depends	3	4	3
Not too much involved	45	44	62
Other responses	10	8	11
	100%	100%	100%
Number of cases	857	217	34

Table B-55

RELATION OF RACE TO U.S. INVOLVEMENT IN
WORLD AFFAIRS

	White	Negro
Too much involved	42%	42%
Pro-con, depends	3	2
Not too much involved	47	33
Other responses	8	23
	100%	100%
Number of cases	1022	103

138

Table B-56

RELATION OF SIZE OF COMMUNITY TO U.S. INVOLVEMENT
IN WORLD AFFAIRS

	Metro centers	Metro suburbs	City or town	Open country
Too much involved	46%	41%	40%	43%
Pro-con, depends	2	2	2	5
Not too much involved	41	50	49	39
Other responses	11	7	9	13
	100%	100%	100%	100%
Number of cases	169	150	601	219

Table B-57

RELATION OF EDUCATION TO U.S. INVOLVEMENT
IN WORLD AFFAIRS

	Grade school	High school	College
Too much involved	45%	45%	27%
Pro-con, depends	3	3	3
Not too much involved	36	46	67
Other responses	16	6	3
	100%	100%	100%
Number of cases	416	517	202

Table B-58

RELATION OF OCCUPATION OF FAMILY HEAD TO U.S. INVOLVEMENT
IN WORLD AFFAIRS

	Professional, business	Clerical, sales	Skilled labor	Unskilled labor	Farm operators
Too much involved	33%	28%	47%	47%	38%
Pro-con, depends	3	--	2	3	8
Not too much involved	56	66	44	36	40
Other responses	8	6	7	14	14
	100%	100%	100%	100%	100%
Number of cases	246	102	337	144	104

Table B-59

RELATION OF LABOR UNION AFFILIATION TO
U.S. INVOLVEMENT IN WORLD AFFAIRS

| | Total population | | Laborers only | |
	Union member	Non- member	Union member	Non- member
Too much involved	44%	41%	46%	48%
Pro-con, depends	4	3	4	1
Not too much involved	44	47	41	42
Other responses	8	9	9	9
	100%	100%	100%	100%
Number of cases	316	808	240	235

Table B-60

RELATION OF INCOME TO U.S. INVOLVEMENT
IN WORLD AFFAIRS

	Under $3000	$3000- 6000	Over $6000
Too much involved	44%	44%	35%
Pro-con, depends	4	2	3
Not too much involved	38	47	57
Other responses	14	7	5
	100%	100%	100%
Number of cases	367	489	240

Table B-61

ATTITUDES TOWARD U.S. INVOLVEMENT IN WORLD AFFAIRS

"Some people think that since the end of the last world war this country has gone too far in concerning itself with problems in other parts of the world. How do you feel about this?"

Response	1948	1952	1954
Agree with statement	32%	55%	41%
Pro-con, depends	2	2	3
Disagree with statement	53	32	46
Other responses	13	11	10
	100%	100%	100%
Number of cases	605	1799	1139

Table B-62

ATTITUDES TOWARD SOCIAL LEGISLATION AMONG MEN AND WOMEN

	Men	Women
Need more social legislation	26%	26%
Doing about right	46	47
Need less social legislation	10	8
Other responses	18	19
	100%	100%
Number of cases	532	607

141

Table B-63

RELATION OF AGE TO SOCIAL LEGISLATION

	21-34	35-54	Over 55
Need more social legislation	29%	25%	27%
Doing about right	46	49	44
Need less social legislation	5	11	11
Other responses	20	15	18
	100%	100%	100%
Number of cases	366	485	281

Table B-64

RELATION OF RELIGION TO SOCIAL LEGISLATION

	Protestant	Catholic	Jewish
Need more social legislation	24%	29%	41%
Doing about right	48	44	41
Need less social legislation	10	8	--
Other responses	18	19	18
	100%	100%	100%
Number of cases	857	217	34

Table B-65

RELATION OF RACE TO SOCIAL LEGISLATION

	White	Negro
Need more social legislation	25%	41%
Doing about right	47	42
Need less social legislation	10	1
Other responses	18	16
	100%	100%
Number of cases	1022	103

Table B-66

RELATION OF SIZE OF COMMUNITY
TO SOCIAL LEGISLATION

	Metro centers	Metro suburbs	City or town	Open country
Need more social legis-lation	41%	29%	24%	17%
Doing about right	40	45	46	54
Need less social legis-lation	5	11	10	8
Other responses	14	15	20	21
	100%	100%	100%	100%
Number of cases	169	150	601	219

Table B-67

RELATION OF EDUCATION TO SOCIAL LEGISLATION

	Grade school	High school	College
Need more social legislation	26%	30%	18%
Doing about right	48	47	42
Need less social legislation	6	8	19
Other responses	20	15	21
	100%	100%	100%
Number of cases	416	517	202

Table B-68

RELATION OF OCCUPATION OF FAMILY HEAD TO
SOCIAL LEGISLATION

	Professional, business	Clerical, sales	Skilled labor	Unskilled labor	Farm operators
Need more social legislation	23%	21%	33%	33%	11%
Doing about right	42	42	48	44	58
Need less social legislation	15	17	4	3	13
Other responses	20	20	15	20	18
	100%	100%	100%	100%	100%
Number of cases	246	102	337	144	104

143

Table B-69

RELATION OF LABOR UNION AFFILIATION
TO SOCIAL LEGISLATION

	Total population		Laborers only	
	Union member	Non-member	Union member	Non-member
Need more social legislation	36%	22%	35%	30%
Doing about right	44	48	46	48
Need less social legislation	4	11	3	4
Other responses	16	19	16	18
	100%	100%	100%	100%
Number of cases	316	808	240	235

Table B-70

RELATION OF INCOME TO SOCIAL LEGISLATION

	Under $3000	$3000-6000	Over $6000
Need more social legislation	27%	27%	23%
Doing about right	49	48	41
Need less social legislation	7	8	16
Other responses	17	17	20
	100%	100%	100%
Number of cases	367	489	240

Table B-71

ATTITUDES TOWARD SOCIAL LEGISLATION

"Some people think the national government should do more
  in trying to deal with such problems as unemployment,
  education, housing, and so on.   Others think that the
  government is already doing too much.   On the whole
  would you say that what the government is doing is
  about right, too much, or not enough?"

	October 1952	October 1954
Should do more	18%	26%
Is doing about right	47	46
Should do less	16	10
More in some areas, less in others	11	10
Other responses	8	8
	100%	100%
Number of cases	1799	1139

Table B-72

ATTITUDES TOWARD SENATOR McCARTHY AMONG MEN AND WOMEN

	Men	Women	Total
Pro-McCarthy	14%	9%	12%
Neutral	43	43	43
Anti-McCarthy	36	38	37
Other responses	7	10	8
	100%	100%	100%
Number of cases	532	607	1139

145

Table B-73

RELATION OF AGE TO ATTITUDE
TOWARD SENATOR McCARTHY

	21-34	35-54	Over 55
Pro-McCarthy	10%	12%	13%
Neutral	48	42	40
Anti-McCarthy	35	38	37
Other responses	7	8	10
	100%	100%	100%
Number of cases	366	485	281

Table B-74

RELATION OF RELIGION TO ATTITUDE
TOWARD SENATOR McCARTHY

	Protestant	Catholic	Jewish
Pro-McCarthy	9%	21%	6%
Neutral	43	48	29
Anti-McCarthy	39	24	53
Other responses	9	7	12
	100%	100%	100%
Number of cases	857	217	34

Table B-75

RELATION OF RACE TO ATTITUDE
TOWARD SENATOR McCARTHY

	White	Negro
Pro-McCarthy	12%	4%
Neutral	42	49
Anti-McCarthy	39	24
Other responses	7	23
	100%	100%
Number of cases	1022	103

146

Table B-76

RELATION OF SIZE OF COMMUNITY TO ATTITUDE TOWARD SENATOR McCARTHY

	Metro centers	Metro suburbs	City or town	Open country
Pro-McCarthy	15%	14%	11%	8%
Neutral	36	45	42	50
Anti-McCarthy	38	36	39	30
Other responses	11	5	8	12
	100%	100%	100%	100%
Number of cases	169	150	601	219

Table B-77

RELATION OF EDUCATION TO ATTITUDE TOWARD SENATOR McCARTHY

	Grade school	High school	College
Pro-McCarthy	9%	13%	14%
Neutral	47	43	37
Anti-McCarthy	29	40	46
Other responses	15	4	3
	100%	100%	100%
Number of cases	416	517	202

Table B-78

RELATION OF OCCUPATION OF FAMILY HEAD TO ATTITUDE TOWARD SENATOR McCARTHY

	Professional, business	Clerical, sales	Skilled labor	Unskilled labor	Farm operators
Pro-McCarthy	13%	9%	9%	13%	8%
Neutral	38	42	43	48	57
Anti-McCarthy	43	43	39	29	25
Other responses	6	6	9	10	10
	100%	100%	100%	100%	100%
Number of cases	246	102	337	144	104

147

Table B-79

RELATION OF LABOR UNION AFFILIATION TO
ATTITUDE TOWARD SENATOR McCARTHY

| | Total population | | Laborers only | |
	Union member	Non-member	Union member	Non-member
Pro-McCarthy	10%	12%	10%	10%
Neutral	42	44	44	46
Anti-McCarthy	43	34	40	31
Other responses	5	10	6	13
	100%	100%	100%	100%
Number of cases	316	808	240	235

Table B-80

RELATION OF INCOME TO ATTITUDE TOWARD
SENATOR McCARTHY

	Under $3000	$3000-6000	Over $6000
Pro-McCarthy	9%	12%	14%
Neutral	44	44	39
Anti-McCarthy	31	39	45
Other responses	16	5	2
	100%	100%	100%
Number of cases	367	489	240

148

Table B-81

RELATION OF PARTY IDENTIFICATION TO ATTITUDE TOWARD SENATOR McCARTHY AMONG PROTESTANTS AND CATHOLICS

	Protestants					Catholics				
	SD	WD	Ind	WR	SR	SD	WD	Ind	WR	SR
Pro-McCarthy	7%	6%	7%	11%	23%	18%	19%	23%	20%	39%
Neutral	34	44	47	48	44	47	53	53	48	33
Anti-McCarthy	55	45	35	33	28	33	21	20	28	23
Other responses	4	5	11	8	5	2	7	4	4	5
	100%	100%	100%	100%	100%	100%	100%	100%	100%	100%
Number of cases	184	213	173	128	123	51	58	55	25	18

149